Hot KNITS

30 COOL, FUN DESIGNS TO KNIT AND WEAR

MELISSA LEAPMAN

PHOTOGRAPHY BY JOE VANDEHATERT

WATSON-GUPTILL PUBLICATIONS / NEW YORK

FOR KPJ

Senior Acquisitions Editor: Joy Aquilino
Project Editor: Andrea Curley
Book Designer: Barbara Balch
Production Manager: Ellen Greene
Principal photography: Joe VanDeHatert
Sweater closeups and details photography: Jacob Hand
Charts and illustrations: Melissa Leapman

First published in 2004 by Watson-Guptill Publications,
a division of VNU Business Media, Inc.,
770 Broadway, New York, N.Y. 10003
www.watsonguptill.com

Library of Congress Cataloging-in-Publication Data
Leapman, Melissa.
Hot knits : 30 cool, fun designs to knit and wear / Melissa Leapman;
photography by Joe VanDeHatert.
p. cm.
ISBN 0-8230-2338-9
1. Knitting. 2. Knitting—Patterns. I. Title.
TT820.L387 2004
746.43'20432—dc22

2003026772

Manufactured in China

First printing, 2004

2 3 4 5 6 7 8 9 / 13 12 11 10 09 08 07 06 05 04

ACKNOWLEDGMENTS

I'd like to thank the following knitters for creating samples and testing patterns for
this book: Helen Borga, Marie Butkowski, Toni Gill, Cindy Grosch, JoAnn Moss,
Joan Murphy, Holly Neiding, Laura Polley, Rusty Slabinski, and Scarlet Taylor. Your
collective expertise (not to mention good humor) made this project possible and lots
of fun!

Many thanks, too, go to the many yarn and button companies that supplied the
beautiful materials used to create these sweaters. Season after season, year after year,
you all have both supported and inspired me!

I am most grateful to my wonderful editors, Joy Aquilino and Andrea Curley, whose
professionalism and extraordinary dedication to this project helped transform my
original vision into reality.

Finally, I wish to express my heartfelt appreciation to all the participants in the knitting
and design workshops I teach across the country. Your enthusiasm and creativity
encourage more of the same in me! Thank you.

Abbreviations

approx — approximately

beg — begin(ning)

BO — bind off

cn — cable needle

CO — cast on

cont — continu(e)(ing)

dec — decreas(e)(ing)

inc — increas(e)(ing)

K — knit

K2tog — knit two stitches together in their front loops as one stitch

K3tog — knit three stitches together in their front loops as one stitch

LH — left-hand

mm — millimeter(s)

mult — multiple(s)

oz — ounces

P — purl

patt(s) — pattern(s)

rem — remain(ing)

RH — right-hand

rnd — round(s)

RS — right side

SSK — slip the first and second stitches one at a time knitwise, then insert point of left-hand needle into the fronts of these stitches and knit them together from this position

SSSK — slip the first, second, and third stitches one at a time knitwise, then insert point of left-hand needle into the fronts of these stitches and knit them together from this position

st(s) — stitch(es)

tog — together

WS — wrong side

yd — yards

* — repeat instructions after asterisk or between asterisks across row or for as many times as instructed

( ) — repeat instructions within parentheses for as many times as instructed

____ — place holder for size(s) to which specific instructions do not pertain

Contents

Abbreviations *3*
Introduction *6*

Introduction

Trend watchers have finally proclaimed what many of us have known all along: **Knitting is HOT!**

Hand-knits are everywhere: on the shelves of your favorite boutique, on the pages of leading fashion magazines, on fashion runways, and—if you could sneak a peek—in the models' own duffle bags.

With the **growing passion** for do-it-yourself projects, new and lapsed knitters alike have been lured to the craft. And why not? Knitting offers a soothing break from today's hectic pace. And this expression of individual creativity has triggered a surge in the number of knitting circles (not to mention online communities) and has actually become a social pursuit—a hip, fun, feel-good, look-good, do-good activity. It seems that everyone is discovering the **magic** contained in a couple of needles and a yummy ball of yarn!

Here's my latest collection of **fun, contemporary sweaters** for every season. In putting together this book, I wanted

- to tempt anxious beginners to move beyond the basics *(Scarves, scarves, and more scarves . . . Been there, done that!)*

- to offer seasoned knitters R&R from constantly flexing their technical muscles *(Sometimes we just want to relax and enjoy the clicking of our needles without any pressure to perform knitting gymnastics.)*

- to provide crafty Fashionistas with up-to-the-minute knitting patterns *(Why not make your next fashion fix truly your own?)*

• to fill all of our knitting baskets with projects that are both **fun to make and stylish to wear.** *(Shouldn't we spend our precious knitting time blissfully transforming beautiful yarns into finished clothing that will make us look and feel great?)*

I hope you will have as much fun making and wearing these sweaters as I had designing them for you. These thirty sweaters incorporate **a modern mix** of silhouettes that work in your busy, varied lives—loose and comfortable tunics for daytime, sexy body-skimming knits that are guaranteed to turn heads, and unconstructed, cozy cardigans for snuggling up with a good book (or friend). My goal is to offer you a collection in which the knitting isn't the end—these are sweaters to live in, to welcome into your wardrobe.

Happy knitting!

Jenny

Think you're too busy to knit a fabulous coat? This mohair duster works up in a flash! Super-sized needles and double-strand yarn make it quick and cozy.

GAUGE

In Box St Patt with two strands of yarn held tog, 10 sts and 14 rows = 4". ***To save time, take time to check gauge.***

BOX STITCH PATTERN

(over mult. 4 + 2 sts)

Row 1 (RS): *K2, P2. Repeat from * across, ending row with K2.

Row 2: *P2, K2. Repeat from * across, ending row with P2.

Row 3: As Row 2.

Row 4: As Row 1.

Repeat Rows 1-4 for patt.

STOCKINETTE STITCH PATTERN

(over any number of sts)

Row 1 (RS): Knit across.

Row 2: Purl across.

Repeat Rows 1 and 2 for patt.

GARTER STITCH PATTERN

(over any number of sts)

Patt Row: Knit across.

Repeat Patt Row.

NOTES

Throughout, two strands of yarn are held together.

Throughout, instructions include one selvage st each side; these sts are not reflected in final measurements.

For sweater assembly, refer to the illustration for set-in construction on page 126.

BACK

With two strands of yarn held tog, CO 50 (58, 66, 74) sts. Beg Box St Patt, and work even until piece measures approx 38½" from beg, ending after WS row.

Shape Armholes

BO 3 (4, 5, 6) sts at beg of next two rows, then BO 2 (2, 3, 3) sts at beg of next two rows—40 (46, 50, 56) sts rem.

Dec 1 st each side every row 2 (5, 6, 9) times, then every other row 2 (1, 1, 0) times—32 (34, 36, 38) sts rem.

Cont even until piece measures approx 47 (47½, 48, 48)" from beg, ending after WS row.

Shape Shoulders

BO 4 (5, 5, 6) sts each shoulder edge once, then BO 4 (4, 5, 5) sts each shoulder edge once.

BO rem 16 sts for back of neck.

Pocket Linings (Make two)

With two strands of yarn held tog, CO 12 sts. Work Stockinette St Patt until piece measures approx 7" from beg, ending after WS row. Slip sts onto holder.

LEFT FRONT

With two strands of yarn held tog, CO 26 (30, 34, 38) sts. Beg Box St Patt, and work even until piece measures approx 23½ (24, 24½, 24½)" from beg, ending after WS row.

Place Pocket Lining

Next Row (RS): Work patt as established across first 4 sts, with RS facing, cont Box St Patt across 12 sts of one pocket lining, place next 12 sts of left front onto stitch holder, work to end row.

SKILL LEVEL

Advanced Beginner

SIZES

Small (Medium, Large, Extra-Large). *Instructions are for smallest size, with changes for other sizes noted in parentheses as necessary.*

FINISHED MEASUREMENTS (BUTTONED)

Bust: 38¼ (43¼, 50¼, 57)"
Total length: 48 (48½, 49, 49)"

MATERIALS

S. R. Kertzer's *Naturally Mohair Plus* (heavy worsted weight; 81% mohair/11% wool/8% nylon; each approx 1¾ oz/50 g and 109 yd/100 m), 21 (22, 24, 25) balls Boysenberry #23

One pair of size 11 (8 mm) knitting needles or size needed to obtain gauge

Stitch holders

Five (five, five, six) 1⅛" buttons (JHB International's *Toluca*, Style #32847 was used on sample garment)

Cont even in patt as established until piece measures same as back to underarm, ending after WS row.

Shape Armhole

BO 3 (4, 5, 6) sts at beg of next row—23 (26, 29, 32) sts rem.

Work one row even.

BO 2 (2, 3, 3) sts at beg of next row—21 (24, 26, 29) sts rem.

Dec 1 st at armhole edge every row 2 (5, 6, 9) times, then every other row 2 (1, 1, 0) times—17 (18, 19, 20) sts rem.

Cont even until piece measures approx 45 (45½, 46, 46)" from beg, ending after RS row.

Shape Neck

Next Row (WS): BO 6 sts at beg of next row—11 (12, 13, 14) sts rem.

Dec 1 st at neck edge every row twice, then every other row once—8 (9, 10, 11) sts rem.

Cont even, if necessary, until piece measures same as back to shoulder, ending after WS row.

Shape Shoulder

BO 4 (5, 5, 6) sts at shoulder edge once, then BO 4 (4, 5, 5) sts at shoulder edge once.

Place markers for five (five, five, six) evenly spaced buttons, making the first one 20 (20½, 21, 21)" from the bottom and the last one ¾" from beg of neck shaping.

RIGHT FRONT

Same as left front *except* reverse all shaping, and make buttonholes on RS rows opposite markers as follows: Work 2 sts in patt as established, BO next 2 sts, work to end row. On subsequent rows, CO 2 sts over the bound-off sts and work them in patt as established.

SLEEVES

With two strands of yarn held tog, CO 34 sts. Beg Box St Patt, and work even until piece measures approx 7½" from beg, ending after WS row.

Inc 1 st each side every thirtieth (twenty-second, sixteenth, sixteenth) row 1 (2, 3, 3) times—36 (38, 40, 40) sts.

Cont even until piece measures approx 20½ (20½, 21½, 21½)" from beg, ending after WS row.

Shape Cap

BO 3 (4, 5, 6) sts at beg of next two rows—30 (30, 30, 28) sts rem.

Dec 1 st each side every fourth row 0 (0, 1, 2) times, every other row 7 (8, 6, 4) times, then every row 1 (0, 1, 1) time—14 sts rem.

BO 2 sts at beg of next four rows—6 sts rem.

BO.

FINISHING

Sew shoulder seams.

Collar

With RS facing and two strands of yarn held tog, pick up and knit 38 sts around neckline, beg and end 2½" in from front neck edges. Beg Box St Patt, and inc 1 st each side every other row six times, working new sts into Box St Patt—50 sts total.

BO.

HOT TIP

When knitting with two strands of yarn at once, don't rewind the individual balls into one big ball. Inevitably, one strand becomes longer than the other, creating a long, unworkable loop of yarn—and lots of unnecessary frustration!

POCKET EDGINGS

With RS facing and two strands of yarn held tog, pick up and knit sts from pocket holder, dec 1 st at center of pocket—11 sts rem. Work Garter St for 1". BO. Sew linings to WS of fronts. Sew sides of pocket edgings to RS of front.

Set in sleeves.

Sew side and sleeve seams, working seam on RS for first 7" of sleeves for fold-up cuffs.

Sew on buttons.

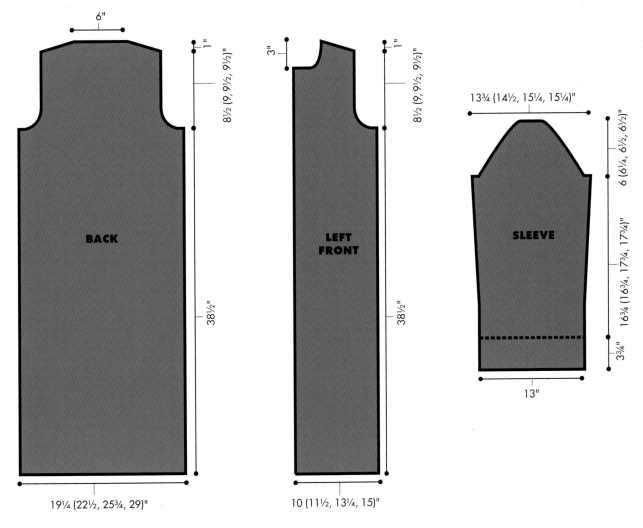

Mackenzie
Keep it simple . . . and sweet!

Pretty little ruffles trim this tapered, easy-to-knit pullover.

GAUGE

In Stockinette St Patt, 20 sts and 28 rows = 4". **To save time, take time to check gauge.**

RUFFLE BORDER PATTERN

(over mult. 6 + 3 sts)

Row 1 (RS): K3, *P3, K3. Repeat from * across.

Row 2: P3, *K3, P3. Repeat from * across.

Repeat Rows 1 and 2 for patt.

STOCKINETTE STITCH PATTERN

(over any number of sts)

Row 1 (RS): Knit across.

Row 2: Purl across.

Repeat Rows 1 and 2 for patt.

K3 P3 RIB PATTERN

(over mult. of 6 sts)

Patt Rnd (RS): *K3, P3. Repeat from * around.

Repeat Patt Rnd.

NOTES

For Body Inc Row: K26 (28, 30, 32, 34) sts, M1, knit across until 26 (28, 30, 32, 34) sts rem in row, ending row with M1, K26 (28, 30, 32, 34).

For Sleeve Inc Row: K3, M1, knit across until 3 sts rem in row, ending row with M1, K3.

For fully-fashioned decreases:
on RS rows: K3, SSK, work across in patt as established until 5 sts rem in row, ending row with K2tog, K3;
on WS rows: P3, P2tog, work across in patt as established until 5 sts rem in row, ending row with P2tog *through their back loops*, P3.

SSK = Slip next 2 sts knitwise one at a time, then insert LH needle into the fronts of these 2 sts and knit them tog from this position.

M1 = Insert LH needle under the horizontal thread that is between st just worked and the next st, and knit into the back of it.

For sweater assembly, refer to the illustration for set-in construction on page 126.

For sweater assembly, refer to the illustration for set-in construction on page 126.

SKILL LEVEL
Advanced Beginner

SIZES
Extra-Small (Small, Medium, Large, Extra-Large). *Instructions are for smallest size, with changes for other sizes noted in parentheses as necessary.*

FINISHED MEASUREMENTS
Bust: 34 (36, 39, 42, 46)"
Total length: 20 (20½, 21, 21½, 22)"

MATERIALS
Westminster Fibers/Jaeger's *Mohair Art* (light worsted weight; 50% mohair/ 50% nylon; each approx 1¾ oz/50 g and 164 yd/ 150 m), 5 (6, 6, 7, 8) balls Red Pepper #607

One pair of size 6 (4 mm) knitting needles or size needed to obtain gauge

Size 6 (4 mm) circular knitting needle, 16" long

Work Body Inc Row on next row.

Work even for eleven more rows.

Work Body Inc Row on next row and then every fourteenth row three times—85 (89, 97, 105, 115) sts.

Work even until piece measures approx 12" from cast-on edge, ending after WS row.

Shape Armholes
BO 4 (5, 6, 7, 8) sts at beg of next two rows, then BO 2 (2, 2, 3, 3) sts at beg of next two rows—73 (75, 81, 85, 93) sts rem.

Work fully-fashioned decreases every row 2 (1, 2, 2, 7) times, then every other row 4 (5, 5, 5, 3) times— 61 (63, 67, 71, 73) sts rem.

Cont even until piece measures approx 18½ (19, 19½, 20, 20½)" from cast-on edge, ending after WS row.

Shape Neck
Next Row (RS): K15 (16, 18, 20, 21) sts; join second ball of yarn and BO middle 31 sts, work to end row.

Work both sides at once with separate balls of yarn and dec 1 st each neck edge every row twice—13 (14, 16, 18, 19) sts rem each side.

Shape Shoulders
BO 3 (4, 4, 5, 5) sts each shoulder edge three times, then BO 4 (2, 4, 3, 4) sts each shoulder edge once.

BACK
CO 225 (237, 261, 285, 315) sts. Work Ruffle Border Patt until piece measures approx 1½" from beg, ending after RS row.

Next Row (WS): P3tog, *K3tog, P3tog. Repeat from * across—75 (79, 87, 95, 105) sts rem.

Beg Stockinette St Patt, and work even for twelve rows.

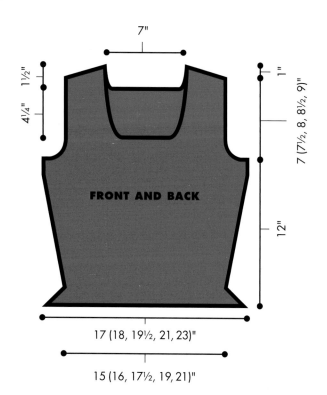

FRONT AND BACK

7"

1½"

4¼"

1"

7 (7½, 8, 8½, 9)"

12"

17 (18, 19½, 21, 23)"

15 (16, 17½, 19, 21)"

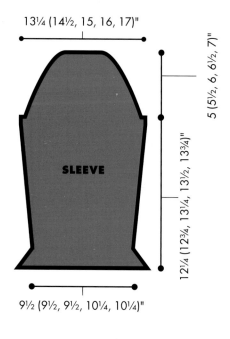

SLEEVE

13¼ (14½, 15, 16, 17)"

5 (5½, 6, 6½, 7)"

12¼ (12¾, 13¼, 13½, 13¾)"

9½ (9½, 9½, 10¼, 10¼)"

FRONT

Same as back until piece measures approx 14¼ (14¾, 15¼, 15¾, 16¼)" from cast-on edge, ending after WS row.

Shape Neck

Next Row (RS): K24 (25, 27, 29, 30) sts; join second ball of yarn and BO middle 13 sts, cont patt as established to end row.

Work both sides at once with separate balls of yarn, and BO 3 sts each neck edge once, then BO 2 sts each neck edge twice—17 (18, 20, 22, 23) sts rem each side.

Work both sides at once with separate balls of yarn and dec 1 st each neck edge every row twice, then every other row twice—13 (14, 16, 18, 19) sts rem each side.

Cont even, if necessary, until piece measures same as back to shoulders, ending after WS row.

Shape Shoulders

Same as back.

SLEEVES

CO 141 (141, 141, 153, 153) sts. Work Ruffle Border Patt until piece measures approx 1½" from beg, ending after RS row.

Next Row (WS): P3tog, *K3tog, P3tog. Repeat from * across—47 (47, 47, 51, 51) sts rem.

Beg Stockinette St Patt, and work Sleeve Inc Row every fourth row 0 (3, 4, 6, 12) times, then every sixth row 6 (10, 10, 9, 5) times, then every eighth row 4 (0, 0, 0, 0) times—67 (73, 75, 81, 85) sts.

Cont even until piece measures approx 12¼ (12¾, 13¼, 13½, 13¾)" from cast-on edge, ending after WS row.

Shape Cap

BO 4 (5, 6, 7, 8) sts at beg of next two rows—59 (63, 63, 67, 69) sts rem.

Work fully-fashioned decreases each side every other row 10 (10, 14, 16, 19) times, then every row 9 (11, 7, 7, 5) times—21 sts rem.

BO 2 sts at beg of next four rows—13 sts rem.

BO.

HOT TIP

For a look that's more everyday, omit the ruffled borders. Instead, knit a simple ribbed edge for 1½ inches. Instructions for basic K1 P1 Rib Pattern are included in the pattern for Jocelyn on page 21.

FINISHING

Sew shoulder seams.

Neckband

With RS facing and circular needle, pick up and knit 102 sts around neckline. Join.

Beg K3 P3 Rib Patt, and work even until band measures approx 1" from beg.

BO *loosely*.

Set in sleeves. Sew sleeve and side seams.

Angela

Looking for some instant drama? Knit this pullover in almost no time at all! Worked cuff-to-cuff, its simple ribbed fabric looks fresher than ever. Talk about knitting with a new angle. . . .

GAUGE

In Rib Patt, 12 sts and 11 rows = 4". ***To save time, take time to check gauge.***

RIB PATTERN

(over mult. 4 + 2 sts)

Row 1 (RS): P2, *K2, P2. Repeat from * across.

Row 2: K2, *P2, K2. Repeat from * across.

Repeat Rows 1 and 2 for patt.

NOTES

Constructionwise, this design is made all in one piece, beginning and ending at sleeve cuffs.

Because this design is worked sideways, row gauge is particularly important.

Throughout, instructions include one selvage st each side; these sts are not reflected in final measurements.

M1 = Insert LH needle under the horizontal thread that is between st just worked and the next st, and knit into the back of it.

SSK = Slip next 2 sts knitwise one at a time, then insert LH needle into the fronts of these 2 sts and knit them tog from this position.

RIGHT SLEEVE

Beg at right sleeve cuff edge, and CO 30 (30, 34, 34) sts. Beg Rib Patt, and work even until piece measures approx 1" from beg, ending after WS row.

Inc Row (RS): P2, K2, place marker, M1, cont patt as established until 4 sts rem in row, ending row with M1, place marker, K2, P2—32 (32, 36, 36) sts.

Inc 1 st after first marker and before second marker every other row 0 (1, 1, 2) more times, then every fourth row 11 (10, 10, 9) times, working new sts into Rib Patt—54 (54, 58, 58) sts.

Cont even, knitting the knit sts and purling the purl sts, until piece measures approx 18¾ (18½, 18¼, 17½)" from beg, ending after WS row.

Place markers at beg and end of last row for side seams.

SKILL LEVEL

Intermediate

SIZES

Small (Medium, Large, Extra-Large). *Instructions are for smallest size, with changes for other sizes noted in parentheses as necessary.*

FINISHED MEASUREMENTS

Bust: 37 (40, 43, 46)"
Total length: 18½ (19, 19¾, 20½)"

MATERIALS

Rowan/Westminster Fibers's *Rowan Big Wool* (bulky weight; 100% merino wool; each approx 3½ oz/ 100 g and 87 yds/80 m), 10 (11, 12, 14) balls Smitten Kitten #03

One pair of size 17 (12.75 mm) knitting needles or size needed to obtain gauge

Stitch markers

Stitch holder

BODY

Beg Back and Front

Next Row (RS): CO 28 (30, 30, 32) sts, then beg with purl (knit, knit, purl) first 2 sts, work in Rib Patt across these new sts and across rest of row—82 (84, 88, 90) sts.

Next Row (WS): CO 28 (30, 30, 32) sts, then beg with knit (purl, purl, knit) first 2 sts, work in patt across these new sts and across rest of row—110 (114, 118, 122) sts.

Cont even in patt until piece measures approx 5¾ (6½, 7¼, 8)" from side seam markers, ending after WS row.

Divide for Neck

Next Row (RS): Work 52 (54, 56, 58) sts in patt as established and place onto holder for front, BO 3 sts, and work to end row—55 (57, 59, 61) sts.

Work even on these 55 (57, 59, 61) back sts in patt as established until there are twenty-one total rows in back neck, ending after RS row. Do not cut yarn. Slip these sts onto holder.

With WS facing, join second ball of yarn, return to 52 (54, 56, 58) sts on holder for front, cont patt as established. Dec 1 st at neck edge on next row and every other row two more times—49 (51, 53, 55) sts.

Work even on these 49 (51, 53, 55) front sts in patt as established for nine rows. Inc 1 st at neck edge on next row then every other row twice more—52 (54, 56, 58) sts.

Join Front and Back

Next Row (WS): Work 55 (57, 59, 61) back sts, CO 3 sts at neck edge, work 52 (54, 56, 58) front sts—110 (114, 118, 122) sts.

Cont even in patt as established until piece measures approx 18½ (20, 21½, 23)" from side seam markers, ending after WS row.

BO 28 (30, 30, 32) sts at beg of next two rows—54 (54, 58, 58) sts.

Place markers at beg and end of last row for side seams.

LEFT SLEEVE

Work in patt as established for approx 1 (1½, 1¼, 1)", ending after WS row.

Dec Row (RS): P2, K1, SSK, cont in patt as established until 5 sts rem in row, ending row with K2tog, K1, P2—52 (52, 56, 56) sts.

Work Dec Row every fourth row 11 (10, 10, 9) times, then every other row 0 (1, 1, 2) times—30 (30, 34, 34) sts.

Work even until piece measures approx 18¾ (18½, 18¼, 17½)" from second side seam markers.

BO in rib.

FINISHING
Neckband

CO 11 sts.

Row 1 (RS): P1, *K2, P2. Repeat from * across, ending row with K2.

Row P2, *K2, P2. Repeat from * across, ending row with K1.

Repeat Rows 1 and 2 until band, when slightly stretched, fits around neckline.

BO in rib.

Sew P1 edge of neckband to neckline, grafting cast-on and bind-off edges at center back of neck.

Sew side and sleeve seams.

HOT TIP

The front neck shaping of this sweater requires that you cast on some stitches in the middle of a row, a technique that might seem awkward at first. I do it using a knit-on cast-on. Here's how: Turn work, *insert RH needle into the first stitch on the LH needle, knit a stitch and immediately transfer it back to the LH needle. Repeat from * until the required number of stitches is cast on, then turn work, and continue across row.

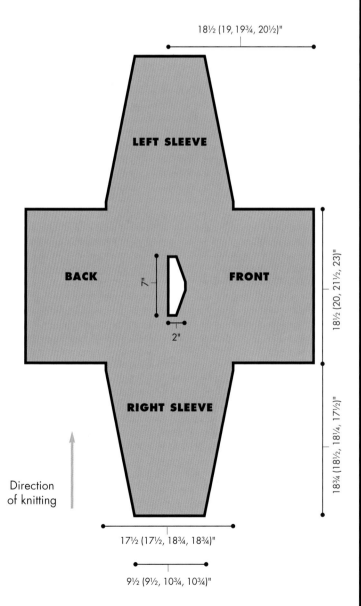

18½ (19, 19¾, 20½)"

LEFT SLEEVE

BACK   FRONT

7"

2"

18½ (20, 21½, 23)"

RIGHT SLEEVE

18¾ (18½, 18¼, 17½)"

Direction of knitting

17½ (17½, 18¾, 18¾)"

9½ (9½, 10¾, 10¾)"

Jocelyn

Soft, sexy, and fun! You'll love wearing— and knitting—this cozy pullover with its flared cuffs, contoured body shaping, and luscious, plush-to-the-touch yarn.

GAUGE

In Stockinette St Patt, 15 sts and 22 rows = 4". ***To save time, take time to check gauge.***

K1 P1 RIB PATTERN

(over mult. 2 sts)

Row 1 (RS): *K1, P1. Repeat from * across.

Patt Row: As Row 1.

Repeat Patt Row for patt.

STOCKINETTE STITCH PATTERN

(over any number of sts)

Row 1 (RS): Knit across.

Row 2: Purl across.

Repeat Rows 1 and 2 for patt.

NOTES

M1 = Insert LH needle under the horizontal thread that is between st just worked and the next st, and knit into the back of it.

SSK = Slip next 2 sts knitwise one at a time, then insert LH needle into the fronts of these 2 sts and knit them tog from this position.

For fully-fashioned increases: K3, M1, knit across until 3 sts rem in row, ending row with M1, K3.

For fully-fashioned decreases: K3, SSK, knit across until 5 sts rem in row, ending row with K2tog, K3.

For sweater assembly, refer to the illustration for set-in construction on page 126.

BACK

CO 66 (72, 78, 84, 90) sts. Beg K1 P1 Rib Patt, and work even until piece measures approx 1" from beg, ending after WS row.

Beg Stockinette St Patt, and work even until piece measures approx 2½ (2½, 3, 3, 3)" from beg, ending after WS row.

Decrease for Waist

Next Row (RS): Knit across, and work fully-fashioned decreases on each side.

Work five rows even.

Work fully-fashioned decreases on each side on next row and then every fourth row four more times—54 (60, 66, 72, 78) sts rem.

Cont even in Stockinette St Patt until piece measures approx 10 (10, 10½, 10½, 11)" from beg, ending after WS row.

Increase for Bust

Work fully-fashioned increases on each side on next row and every fourth row three more times, then every sixth row twice—66 (72, 78, 84, 90) sts.

SKILL LEVEL

Intermediate

SIZES

Extra-Small (Small, Medium, Large, Extra-Large). *Instructions are for smallest size, with changes for other sizes noted in parentheses as necessary.*

FINISHED MEASUREMENTS

Bust: 35 (38½, 42, 45, 48)"
Total length: 23½ (24, 24½, 25, 26)"

MATERIALS

JCA/Reynolds's *Paris* (bulky weight; 80% viscose/20% cotton; each approx 1¾ oz/ 50 g and 60 yd/55 m), 14 (16, 17, 19, 20) balls Merlot #69

One pair of size 8 (5 mm) knitting needles or size needed to obtain gauge

Leather lacing, 1 yd

Cont even in Stockinette St Patt until piece measures approx 15½ (15½, 16, 16, 16½)" from beg, ending after WS row.

Shape Armholes

BO 3 (3, 4, 5, 6) sts at beg of next two rows, then BO 2 (2, 3, 3, 3) sts at beg of next two rows—56 (62, 64, 68, 72) sts rem.

Work fully-fashioned decreases each side every row 0 (1, 3, 4, 6) times, then every other row 3 (4, 3, 3, 3) times—50 (52, 52, 54, 54) sts rem.

Cont even until piece measures approx 22½ (23, 23½, 24, 25)" from beg, ending after WS row.

Shape Shoulders

BO 4 sts each shoulder edge twice, then BO 3 (4, 4, 5, 5) sts each shoulder edge once.

BO rem 28 sts for back of neck.

FRONT

Same as back until piece measures approx 15¾ (16¼, 16¾, 17¼, 18¼)" from beg, ending after RS row.

Shape Neck

Next Row (WS): Work across first half of rem sts; join second ball of yarn and work to end row.

Cont armhole shaping same as back, *and at the same time,* work both sides at once with separate balls of

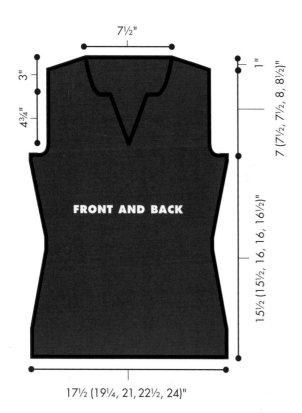

FRONT AND BACK

7½"

3"

4¾"

1"

7 (7½, 7½, 8, 8½)"

15½ (15½, 16, 16, 16½)"

17½ (19¼, 21, 22½, 24)"

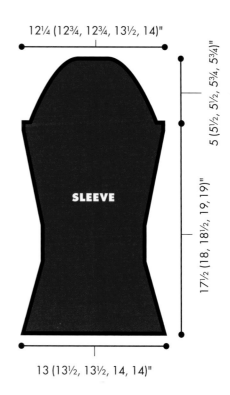

SLEEVE

12¼ (12¾, 12¾, 13½, 14)"

5 (5½, 5½, 5¾, 5¾)"

17½ (18, 18½, 19, 19)"

13 (13½, 13½, 14, 14)"

yarn, and dec 1 st each neck edge every sixth row three times, then every fourth row twice—20 (21, 21, 22, 22) sts rem each side.

BO 2 sts each neck edge twice—16 (17, 17, 18, 18) sts rem each side.

Dec 1 st each neck edge every row three times, then every other row twice—11 (12, 12, 13, 13) sts rem each side. Work even until piece measures same as back to shoulders, ending after WS row.

Shape Shoulders
Same as for back.

Sleeves
CO 48 (50, 50, 52, 52) sts. Beg K1 P1 Rib Patt, and work even until piece measures approx 1" from beg, ending after WS row.

Beg Stockinette St Patt, and work fully-fashioned decreases each side on first row and every sixth row five more times—36 (38, 38, 40, 40) sts rem.

Cont even in Stockinette St Patt until piece measures approx 9 (9, 9, 9½, 9½)" from beg, ending after WS row.

Work fully-fashioned increases each side on next row and every eighth row 4 (2, 1, 0, 4) more times, then every tenth row 0 (2, 3, 4, 1) times—46 (48, 48, 50, 52) sts.

Cont even until piece measures approx 17½ (18, 18½, 19, 19)" from beg, ending after WS row.

Shape Cap
BO 3 (3, 4, 5, 6) sts at beg of next two rows—40 (42, 40, 40, 40) sts rem.

Work fully-fashioned decreases each side on next row and then every fourth row 0 (0, 1, 2, 2) times, then every other row 8 (9, 7, 6, 6) times—22 sts rem.

BO 2 sts at beg of next six rows.

BO rem 10 sts.

FINISHING
Sew shoulder seams.

Neck Edging
With RS facing, beg at top of V-neck opening on right front, and pick up and knit 68 sts along right neck edge, back of neck, and left neck edge, ending at top of V-neck opening on left front.

Next Row: Knit.

Next Row: Knit and BO.

Front V-Neck Edging
With RS facing, beg at top of V-neck opening on left front, and pick up and knit 38 sts along V-neck opening.

Next Row: Knit.

Next Row: Knit and BO.

Set in sleeves. Sew sleeve and side seams.

Lace leather loosely through V-neck opening.

Leah

You'll be amazed at how quickly this design knits up! Elongated stitches—made by wrapping yarn around the knitting needle twice—are the perfect showcase for this beautiful ribbon yarn. Uncomplicated details, such as simple shaping and a mitered square neckline, add to its understated elegance.

GAUGE

In Drop St Cable Patt with larger needles, 22 sts and 24 rows = 4". ***To save time, take time to check gauge.***

GARTER STITCH

(over any number of sts)

Row 1 (RS): Knit across.

Patt Row: As Row 1.

Repeat Patt Row.

DROP STITCH CABLE PATTERN

(mult. 6 + 2 sts)

Row 1 (RS): Knit across.

Row 2: Purl across.

Rows 3 and 4: As Rows 1 and 2.

Row 5: K1, *knit next st *wrapping yarn twice around needle.* Repeat from * across, ending row with K1.

Row 6: K1, *slip next 3 sts onto cn *allowing extra loops to drop,* and hold in front, P3 *allowing extra loops to drop,* P3 from cn. Repeat from * across, ending row with K1.

Repeat Rows 1-6 for patt.

NOTES

In Row 5 of Drop Stitch Cable Patt, elongated sts are formed by wrapping the yarn *twice* around the needle; these extra loops are dropped on the subsequent row.

SSK = Slip next 2 sts knitwise one at a time, then insert LH needle into the fronts of these 2 sts and knit them tog from this position.

Throughout, instructions include one selvage st each side; these sts are not reflected in final measurements.

For sweater assembly, refer to the illustration for square indented construction on page 126.

SKILL LEVEL

Intermediate

SIZES

Extra-Small (Small, Medium, Large, Extra-Large). *Instructions are for smallest size, with changes for other sizes noted in parentheses as necessary.*

FINISHED MEASUREMENTS

Bust: 37 (41½, 46, 50, 54½,)"
Total length: 18 (18½, 18½, 19, 20)"

MATERIALS

Berroco's *Zen* (worsted weight; 60% nylon/40% cotton; each approx 1¾ oz/ 50 g and 110 yd/101 m), 12 (12, 13, 13, 14) hanks Tofu #8201

One pair each of sizes 6 and 8 (4 and 5 mm) knitting needles or size needed to obtain gauge

Cable needle

Stitch markers

Cont even until piece measures approx 9½ (9½, 9½, 9½, 10½)" from beg, ending after WS row.

Shape Armholes
BO 12 (12, 18, 18, 18) sts at beg of next two rows—80 (92, 92, 104, 116) sts rem.

Cont even until piece measures approx 16 (16½, 16½, 17, 18)" from beg, ending after WS row.

Shape Neck
Next Row (RS): Work patt as established across first 20 (26, 26, 32, 38) sts; join second ball of yarn and BO middle 40 sts, work to end row.

Work both sides at once with separate balls of yarn until piece measures approx 18 (18½, 18½, 19, 20)" from beg, ending after WS row.

BO.

FRONT
Same as back until piece measures approx 14 (14½, 14½, 15, 16)" from beg, ending after WS row.

Shape Neck
Next Row (RS): Work patt as established across first 20 (26, 26, 32, 38) sts; join second ball of yarn and BO middle 40 sts, work to end row.

Work both sides at once with separate balls of yarn until piece measures approx 18 (18½, 18½, 19, 20)" from beg, ending after WS row.

BO.

BACK
With smaller needles, CO 88 (98, 109, 119, 129) sts. Beg Garter St Patt, and work even until piece measures approx 1" from beg, ending after RS row.

Next Row (WS): Knit, inc 16 (18, 19, 21, 23) sts evenly across—104 (116, 128, 140, 152) sts.

Change to larger needles and beg Drop St Cable Patt.

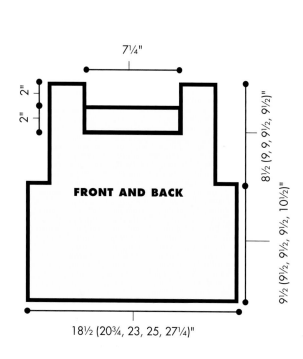

7¼"

2" 2"

2"

FRONT AND BACK

8½ (9, 9, 9½, 9½)"

9½ (9½, 9½, 9½, 10½)"

18½ (20¾, 23, 25, 27¼)"

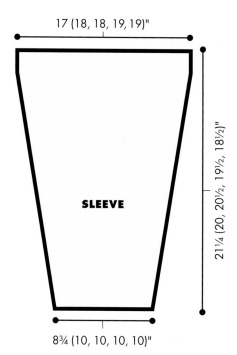

17 (18, 18, 19, 19)"

SLEEVE

21¼ (20, 20½, 19½, 18½)"

8¾ (10, 10, 10, 10)"

SLEEVES

With smaller needles, CO 42 (47, 47, 47, 47) sts. Beg Garter St Patt, and work even until piece measures approx 1" from beg, ending after RS row.

Next Row (WS): Knit, inc 8 (9, 9, 9, 9) sts evenly across—50 (56, 56, 56, 56) sts.

Change to larger needles, beg Drop St Cable Patt, and inc 1 st each side every other row 0 (0, 0, 2, 5) times, then every fourth row 11 (12, 14, 22, 19) times, then every sixth row 11 (9, 7, 0, 0) times—94 (98, 98, 104, 104) sts.

Cont even until piece measures approx 21¼ (20, 20½, 19½, 18½)" from beg, ending after WS row.

BO.

FINISHING

Sew left shoulder seam.

Neckband

With RS facing and smaller needles, beg at right shoulder edge and pick up and knit 11 sts along right back neck edge, place marker, pick up and knit 1 st in corner, place marker, pick up and knit 42 sts along back of neck, place marker, pick up and knit 1 st in corner, place marker, pick up and knit 11 sts to left shoulder seam, pick up and knit 22 sts along left front neck edge, place marker, pick up and knit 1 st in corner, place marker, pick up and knit 42 sts along front neck edge, place marker, pick up and knit 1 st in corner, place marker, pick up and knit 22 sts to right shoulder edge—154 sts total around neckline.

Next Row (WS): *Knit across to next marker, slip marker, P1, slip marker. Repeat from * three more times, ending row with knit sts along right back neck edge to right shoulder.

Next Row (RS): *Knit across to 2 sts before next marker, SSK, slip marker, knit corner st, slip marker, K2tog *through back loops.* Repeat from * three more times, ending row with knit sts along right front neck edge to right shoulder.

Repeat last two rows until band measures approx 1" from beg.

BO.

Sew right shoulder seam, including side of neckband.

Set in sleeves.

Sew sleeve and side seams.

Robin

The geometric pattern in this colorblock pullover is especially fun to do when knitting with beautiful (and forgiving!) merino wool. Toss this sweater over a pair of pants and you're good to go!

GAUGE

In Stockinette St Patt with larger needles, 20 sts and 28 rows = 4". ***To save time, take time to check gauge.***

K2 P2 RIB PATTERN

(over mult. 4 + 2 sts)

Row 1 (RS): K2, *P2, K2. Repeat from * across.

Row 2: P2, *K2, P2. Repeat from * across.

Repeat Rows 1 and 2 for patt.

STOCKINETTE STITCH PATTERN

(over any number of sts)

Row 1 (RS): Knit across.

Row 2: Purl across.

Repeat Rows 1 and 2 for patt.

LOWER COLORBLOCK PATTERN

(over mult. 12 sts)

See chart on page 31.

UPPER COLORBLOCK PATTERN

(over mult. 12 sts)

See chart on page 31.

NOTES

M1 = Insert LH needle under the horizontal thread that is between st just worked and the next st, and knit into the back of it.

SSK = Slip next 2 sts knitwise one at a time, then insert LH needle into the fronts of these 2 sts and knit them tog from this position.

For fully-fashioned decreases:
on RS rows: K1, SSK, work across in patt as established until 3 sts rem in row, ending row with K2tog, K1; *on WS rows:* P1, P2tog, work across in patt as established until 3 sts rem in row, ending row with P2tog *through their back loops*, P1.

When working Lower Colorblock Patt and Upper Colorblock Patt, use intarsia technique.

For sweater assembly, refer to the illustration for set-in construction on page 126.

BACK

With smaller needles and A, CO 86 (98, 110, 122, 134) sts. Beg K2 P2 Rib Patt, and work even until piece measures approx 1½" from beg, ending after WS row.

Change to larger needles, beg Stockinette St Patt, and work even until piece measures approx 5½" from beg, ending after WS row.

Beg Color Pattern

K1 with A, work Row 1 of Lower Colorblock Patt over middle 84 (96, 108, 120, 132) sts, K1 with A to end row.

Cont even in patts as established until Row 12 of Lower Colorblock Patt is completed.

Cont even with C in Stockinette St Patt until piece measures approx 15 (15¼, 15½, 15½, 15½)", ending after WS row.

Shape Armholes

BO 2 (4, 6, 8, 10) sts at beg of next two rows, then BO 2 (3, 3, 4, 5) sts at beg of next two rows—78 (84, 92, 98, 104) sts rem.

SKILL LEVEL
Intermediate

SIZES
Extra-Small (Small, Medium, Large, Extra-Large). *Instructions are for smallest size, with changes for other sizes noted in parentheses as necessary.*

FINISHED MEASUREMENTS
Bust: 34½ (39½, 44, 49, 54)"
Total length: 23½ (24, 24½, 25, 25½)"

MATERIALS
Trendsetter/Lane Borgosesia's *Maratona* (worsted weight; 100% wool; each approx 1¾ oz/ 50 g and 121 yd/110 m), 6 (7, 8, 8, 9) balls Rust Heather #41257 (A), 2 (2, 2, 3, 3) balls Gold #14 (B), and 5 (5, 5, 6, 7) balls Red Clay #8524 (C)

One pair each of sizes 5 and 7 (3.75 and 4.5 mm) knitting needles or size needed to obtain gauge

Work fully-fashioned decreases each side every row 1 (6, 10, 12, 12) times, then every other row 4 (2, 1, 2, 4) times—68 (68, 70, 70, 72) sts rem.

Cont even until piece measures approx 17 (17½, 18, 18½, 19)" from beg, ending after WS row.

Beg Color Pattern
K4 (4, 5, 5, 6) sts with C, work Row 1 of Upper Colorblock Patt over middle 60 sts, K4 (4, 5, 5, 6) sts with C to end row.

Cont patt as established until Row 12 of Upper Colorblock Patt is completed, then cont even with A until piece measures approx 22½ (23, 23½, 24, 24½)" from beg, ending after WS row.

Shape Shoulders
BO 4 (4, 4, 4, 5) sts each shoulder edge three times, then BO 5 (5, 6, 6, 4) sts each shoulder edge once.

BO rem 34 sts for back of neck.

FRONT
Same as back until piece measures approx 21 (21½, 22, 22½, 23)" from beg, ending after WS row.

Shape Neck
Next Row (RS): Work across first 27 (27, 28, 28, 29) sts; join second ball of yarn and BO middle 14 sts, work patt as established to end row.

Work both sides at once with separate balls of yarn, and BO 4 sts each neck edge once, then BO 2 sts each neck edge once.

Dec 1 st each neck edge every row twice, then every other row twice—17 (17, 18, 18, 19) sts rem each side.

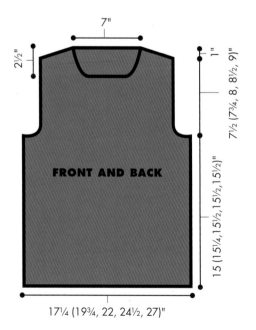

FRONT AND BACK

7"

2½"

1"

7½ (7¾, 8, 8½, 9)"

15 (15¼, 15½, 15½, 15½)"

17¼ (19¾, 22, 24½, 27)"

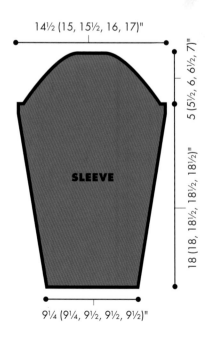

SLEEVE

14½ (15, 15½, 16, 17)"

5 (5½, 6, 6½, 7)"

18 (18, 18½, 18½, 18½)"

9¼ (9¼, 9½, 9½, 9½)"

Cont even until piece measures same as back to shoulders, ending after WS row.

Shape Shoulders
Same as for back.

SLEEVES
With smaller needles and A, CO 46 (46, 48, 48, 48) sts. Beg K2 P2 Rib Patt, and work even until piece measures approx 1½" from beg, ending after WS row.

Change to larger needles, beg Stockinette St Patt, and inc 1 st each side on next row and every fourth row 0 (0, 0, 0, 4) times, then every sixth row 2 (10, 9, 13, 14) times, then every eighth row 10 (4, 5, 2, 0) times, *and at the same time,* set up color charts as follows: After eight (eight, eight, eight, six) rows of A have been completed following K2 P2 Rib Patt, K1 (1, 2, 2, 2) sts with A, repeat Lower Colorblock Patt Row 1 across sts until 1 (1, 2, 2, 2) sts rem in row, ending row with K1 (1, 2, 2, 2) sts with A.

Cont sleeve increases, work Lower Colorblock Patt until Row 12 is completed, then work twenty-eight rows with C—60 (62, 64, 64, 66) sts.

For Size Extra-Small Only:
With C, K6, work Row 1 of Upper Colorblock Patt across until 6 sts rem in row, ending row with K6 sts with C—60 sts.

For Sizes Small, Medium, Large, and Extra-Large Only:
With C, K1, M1, K _ (6, 7, 7, 8) sts, work Row 1 of Upper Colorblock Patt across until _ (7, 8, 8, 9) sts rem in row, ending row with K _ (6, 7, 7, 8) sts with C, M1, K1—_ (64, 66, 66, 68) sts.

For All Sizes:
Cont sleeve increases, work Upper Colorblock Patt until Row 12 is completed, then cont with A—72 (76, 78, 80, 86) sts.

Cont even until sleeve measures approx 18 (18, 18½, 18½, 18½)" from beg, ending after WS row.

Shape Cap
BO 2 (4, 6, 8, 10) sts at beg of next two rows—68 (68, 66, 64, 66) sts rem.

Work fully-fashioned decreases each side every other row 6 (8, 13, 18, 20) times, then every row 18 (16, 10, 4, 3) times—20 sts rem.

BO 2 sts at beg of next four rows.

BO rem 12 sts.

FINISHING
Sew right shoulder seam.

Neckband
With RS facing, smaller needles, and A, pick up and knit 86 sts around neckline. Work even in K2 P2 Rib Patt until band measures approx 4" from beg, ending after WS row. Change to C, and work two more rows of K2 P2 Rib Patt.

BO *loosely* in rib.

Sew left shoulder seam, including side of neckband.

Set in sleeves. Sew sleeve and side seams.

LOWER COLORBLOCK PATTERN

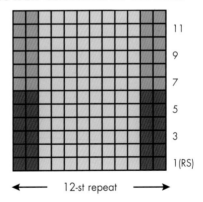

← 12-st repeat →

UPPER COLORBLOCK PATTERN

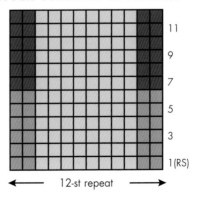

← 12-st repeat →

KEY ■ = A □ = B ▨ = C

Marla

Worked in a surprisingly lightweight cotton-blend yarn, this springtime sweater features an embossed lacy leaf panel that travels up the front and then divides, delicately framing the neckline.

GAUGE

In Garter Ridge Patt with larger needles, 22 sts and 28 rows = 4". ***To save time, take time to check gauge.***

GARTER STITCH PATTERN

(over any number of sts)

Patt Row: Knit.

Repeat Patt Row.

GARTER RIDGE PATTERN

(over any number of sts)

Row 1 (RS): Knit.

Row 2 and all WS rows: Purl.

Rows 3, 5, 7, 9, and 11: As Row 1.

Rows 13 and 14: Purl.

Repeat Rows 1-14 for patt.

LACY CABLE PANEL

(over middle 24 sts)

See chart on page 35.

NOTES

SSSK = Slip next 3 sts knitwise one at a time, then insert LH needle into the fronts of these 3 sts and knit them tog from this position.

SSK = Slip next 2 sts knitwise one at a time, then insert LH needle into the fronts of these 2 sts and knit them tog from this position.

For sweater assembly, refer to the illustration for square indented construction on page 126.

BACK

With smaller needles, CO 83 (90, 100, 110, 120) sts. Work Garter St Patt until piece measures approx 1" from beg, inc 15 (16, 18, 20, 22) sts evenly across last row—98 (106, 118, 130, 142) sts.

Change to larger needles, and set up patts as follows: Work Row 1 of Garter Ridge Patt across first 37 (41, 47, 53, 59) sts, place marker, work Row 1 of Lacy Cable Panel over middle 24 sts, place marker, work Row 1 of Garter Ridge Patt across last 37 (41, 47, 53, 59) sts to end row.

Work even in patts as established until piece measures approx 12" from beg, ending after WS row.

Shape Armholes

Cont patts as established, BO 6 (10, 12, 14, 18) sts at beg of next two rows—86 (86, 94, 102, 106) sts rem.

Cont even in patts as established until piece measures approx 20 (20½, 20½, 21, 21)" from beg, ending after WS row.

Shape Neck

Next Row (RS): Work patts as established across first 15 (15, 19, 23, 25) sts; join second ball of yarn and BO middle 56 sts, work patts as established to end row.

Work both sides at once with separate balls of yarn, and dec 1 st each neck edge every row three times—12 (12, 16, 20, 22) sts rem each side.

Cont even, if necessary, until piece measures approx 20½ (21, 21, 21½, 21½)" from beg, ending after WS row.

Shape Shoulders

BO 3 (3, 4, 5, 5) sts each shoulder edge twice, then BO 3 (3, 4, 5, 6) sts each shoulder edge twice.

FRONT

Same as back until piece measures approx 14½ (15, 15, 15½, 15½)" from beg, ending after WS row.

Shape Neck

Next Row (RS): Work patts as established across first 29 (29, 33, 37, 39) sts, K2tog, place marker, work patt as established across next 12 sts; join second ball of yarn and work patt as established across first 12 sts, place marker, SSK, cont patt as established to end row.

Work both sides at once with separate balls of yarn, and work fully-fashioned decreases in this manner at markers every other row sixteen more times, then every fourth row twice—24 (24, 28, 32, 34) sts rem each side. Cont even until piece measures same as back to shoulders, ending after WS row.

Shape Shoulders

Same as back.

Cont even in Lacy Cable Panel on rem 12 sts each side until neckbands, when slightly stretched, meet at center back of neck.

BO.

SLEEVES

With smaller needles, CO 44 (48, 48, 48, 48) sts. Work Garter St Patt until piece measures approx 1" from beg, inc 8 (8, 8, 9, 9) sts evenly across last row—52 (56, 56, 57, 57) sts.

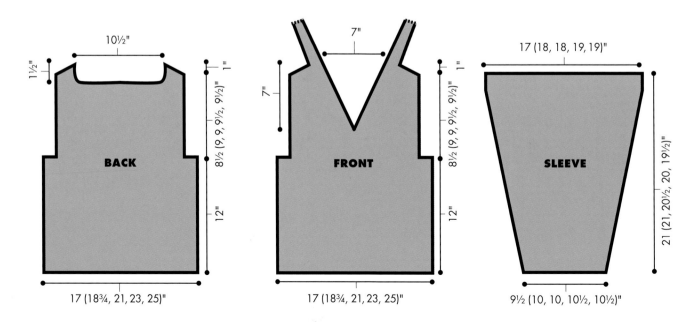

Change to larger needles, beg Garter Ridge Patt, and inc 1 st each side every fourth row 0 (3, 4, 15, 18) times, then every sixth row 17 (19, 18, 9, 6) times, then every eighth row 4 (0, 0, 0, 0) times—94 (100, 100, 105, 105) sts.

Cont even until piece measures approx 21 (21, 20¾, 20, 19½)" from beg, ending after WS row.

BO.

FINISHING

Sew shoulder seams. Sew sides of neckbands to neck-line. Sew bound-off edges of neckbands tog at back of neck.

Set in sleeves. Sew sleeve and side seams.

LACY CABLE PANEL

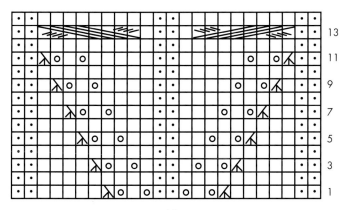

13
11
9
7
5
3
1

Middle 24 sts

KEY

☐ = K on RS; P on WS

· = P on RS; K on WS

⋏ = K3tog

o = Yarn over

⋋ = SSSK

= Slip next 4 sts onto cn and hold in back; K4; K4 from cn

= Slip next 4 sts onto cn and hold in front; K4; K4 from cn

Audrey

Simple rope cables travel up this red-hot cardigan in an hourglass shape. The result? A wardrobe basic that will flatter every figure!

GAUGE

In Stockinette St Patt with larger needles, 13 sts and 20 rows = 4". **To save time, take time to check gauge.**

K2 P2 RIB PATTERN

(over mult. 4 + 2 sts)

Row 1 (RS): K2, *P2, K2. Repeat from * across.

Row 2: P2, *K2, P2. Repeat from * across.

Repeat Rows 1 and 2 for patt.

SIMPLE RIGHT CABLE PANEL

(over 19 sts)

See chart on page 40.

SIMPLE LEFT CABLE PANEL

(over 19 sts)

See chart on page 40.

STOCKINETTE STITCH PATTERN

(over any number of sts)

Row 1 (RS): Knit across.

Row 2: Purl across.

Repeat Rows 1 and 2 for patt.

MEANDERING RIGHT CABLE PANEL

(over 19 sts)

See chart on page 41.

MEANDERING LEFT CABLE PANEL

(over 19 sts)

See chart on page 41.

NOTES

SSK = Slip next 2 sts knitwise one at a time, then insert LH needle into the fronts of these 2 sts and knit them tog from this position.

For fully-fashioned decreases:
on RS rows: K1, SSK, work across in patt as established until 3 sts rem in row, ending row with K2tog, K1; **on WS rows:** P1, P2tog, work across in patt as established until 3 sts rem in row, ending row with P2tog *through their back loops*, P1.

For sweater assembly, refer to the illustration for set-in construction on page 126.

SKILL LEVEL
Advanced

SIZES
Small (Medium, Large, Extra-Large, Extra-Extra Large). *Instructions are for smallest size, with changes for other sizes noted in parentheses as necessary.*

FINISHED MEASUREMENTS
Bust (Buttoned): 33¼ (37, 42, 48, 52½)"
Total length: 24"

MATERIALS
Lion Brand's *Kool Wool* (bulky weight; 50% merino wool/50% acrylic; each approx 1¾ oz/50 g and 60 yd/54 m), 17 (18, 19, 20, 21) balls Tomato Red #113

One pair each of sizes 9 and 10½ (5.5 and 6.5 mm) knitting needles or size needed to obtain gauge

29" Circular knitting needle, size 9 (5.5 mm)

Four 1" buttons (One World Button Supply Company's *Corozo* Style #SPN 106-44TR was used on sample garment)

Stitch markers

Shape Armholes

Next Row (RS): Cont patts as established, BO 3 (3, 5, 7, 9) sts at beg of next two rows—60 (64, 68, 76, 80) sts rem.

Work fully-fashioned decreases each side every row 2 (2, 6, 9, 10) times, then every other row 4 (4, 2, 2, 3) times—48 (52, 52, 54, 54) sts rem—**and at the same time,** when Row 54 of Meandering Right Cable Panel and Meandering Left Cable Panel is completed, set up Simple Right Cable Panel and Simple Left Cable Panel as follows:

Next Row (RS): Maintaining armhole decreases as set, knit across to marker, remove marker, K1, place marker, work Row 1 of Simple Right Cable Panel over next 19 sts, place marker, K8 (12, 12, 14, 14) sts, place marker, work Row 1 of Simple Left Cable Panel over next 19 sts, place marker, K1, remove marker, work across to end row.

Cont even in patts as established until piece measures approx 19¼" from beg, ending after Row 6 of Simple Right Cable Panel and Simple Left Cable Panel.

Next Row (RS): K2, (K2tog) four times, K28 (32, 32, 34, 34) sts, (K2tog) four times, K2 to end row—40 (44, 44, 46, 46) sts rem.

Cont even in Stockinette St Patt until piece measures approx 22½" from beg, ending after WS row.

Shape Neck

Next Row (RS): Knit across first 10 (12, 12, 13, 13) sts, join second ball of yarn and BO middle 20 sts, knit across to end row.

Work both sides at once with separate balls of yarn and dec 1 st each neck edge once—9 (11, 11, 12, 12) sts rem each side.

Cont even until piece measures approx 23" from beg, ending after WS row.

Shape Shoulders

BO 3 (4, 4, 4, 4) sts each shoulder edge twice, then BO 3 (3, 3, 4, 4) sts each shoulder edge once.

LEFT FRONT

With smaller needles, CO 30 (34, 38, 42, 46) sts. Beg K2 P2 Rib Patt, and work even for six rows.

Change to larger needles.

Set Up Patts

Next Row (RS): K10 (10, 14, 19, 23) sts, place marker, work Row 1 of Simple Right Cable Panel over next 19 sts, place marker, K1 (5, 5, 4, 4) sts to end row.

BACK

With smaller needles, CO 66 (70, 78, 90, 98) sts. Beg K2 P2 Rib Patt, and work even for six rows.

Change to larger needles.

Set Up Patts

Next Row (RS): K10 (10, 14, 19, 23) sts, place marker, work Row 1 of Simple Right Cable Panel over next 19 sts, place marker, K8 (12, 12, 14, 14) sts, place marker, work Row 1 of Simple Left Cable Panel over next 19 sts, place marker, K10 (10, 14, 19, 23) sts to end row.

Cont even in patts as established until piece measures approx 4¾" from beg, ending after Row 6 of Simple Right Cable Panel and Simple Left Cable Panel.

Next Row (RS): K9 (9, 13, 18, 22) sts, place marker, work Row 1 of Meandering Right Cable Panel over next 19 sts, place marker, K10 (14, 14, 16, 16) sts, place marker, work Row 1 of Meandering Left Cable Panel over next 19 sts, place marker, K9 (9, 13, 18, 22) sts to end row.

Cont even in patts as established until piece measures approx 14½ (14, 14, 13½, 13½)" from beg, ending after WS row.

Cont even in patts as established until piece measures approx 4¾" from beg, ending after Row 6 of Simple Right Cable Panel.

Next Row (RS): K9 (9, 13, 18, 22) sts, place marker, work Row 1 of Meandering Right Cable Panel over next 19 sts, place marker, K2 (6, 6, 5, 5) sts to end row.

Cont even in patts as established until piece measures approx 14½ (14, 14, 13½, 13½)" from beg, ending after WS row.

Shape Armhole
Next Row (RS): Cont patts as established, BO 3 (3, 5, 7, 9) sts at beg of next row—27 (31, 33, 35, 37) sts rem.

Work fully-fashioned decreases *at armhole edge only* every row 2 (2, 6, 9, 10) times, then every other row 4 (4, 2, 2, 3) times, *and at the same time,* when piece measures approx 16" from beg, ending after RS row, shape neck as follows:

Shape Neck
Cont armhole decreases, work fully-fashioned decreases at neck edge every other row 0 (3, 3, 0, 0) times, every fourth row 7 times, then every sixth row 1 (0, 0, 1, 1) times, *and at the same time,* when Row 54 of Meandering Right Cable Panel is completed, set up Simple Cable Panel as follows:

Next Row (RS): K10 (10, 14, 19, 23) sts, place marker, work Row 1 of Simple Right Cable Panel over next 19 sts, place marker, K1 (5, 5, 4, 4) sts to end row.

Cont decreases and cable panel as established, *and at*

the same time, when piece measures approx 19¼" from beg, ending after Row 6 of Simple Right Cable Panel, decrease as follows:

Next Row (RS): K2, (K2tog) four times, knit across to end row.

Cont even until piece measures approx 23" from beg, ending after WS row.

Shape Shoulders
BO 3 (4, 4, 4, 4) sts at shoulder edge twice. Work one row even. BO 3 (3, 3, 4, 4) sts at beg of next row.

RIGHT FRONT
Same as left front *except* set up patts as follows and reverse all shaping:

Set Up Patts
Next Row (RS): K1 (5, 5, 4, 4), place marker, work Row 1 of Simple Left Cable Panel over next 19 sts, place marker, K10 (10, 14, 19, 23) sts to end row.

SLEEVES
With smaller needles, CO 34 sts. Beg K2 P2 Rib Patt, and work even for six rows.

Change to larger needles, beg Stockinette St Patt, and inc 1 st each side every sixth row 0 (1, 1, 4, 4) times, every eighth row 3 (9, 9, 7, 7) times, then every tenth row 5 (0, 0, 0, 0) times—50 (54, 54, 56, 56) sts.

Work even until piece measures approx 17½ (18, 18, 18½, 18½)" from beg, ending after WS row.

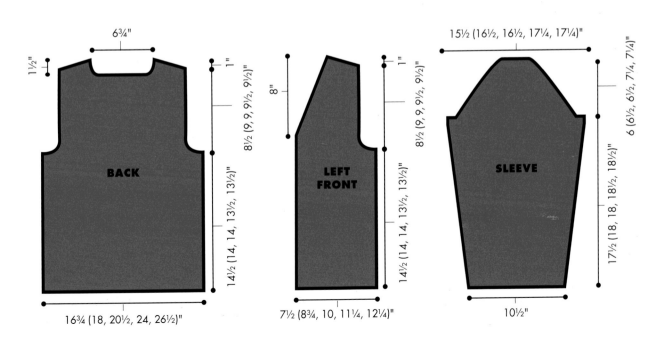

BACK

6¾"
1½"
1"
8½ (9, 9, 9½, 9½)"
14½ (14, 14, 13½, 13½)"
16¾ (18, 20½, 24, 26½)"

LEFT FRONT

8"
1"
8½ (9, 9, 9½, 9½)"
14½ (14, 14, 13½, 13½)"
7½ (8¾, 10, 11¼, 12¼)"

SLEEVE

15½ (16½, 16½, 17¼, 17¼)"
6 (6½, 6½, 7¼, 7¼)"
17½ (18, 18, 18½, 18½)"
10½"

Shape Cap

BO 3 (3, 5, 7, 9) sts at beg of next two rows—44 (48, 44, 42, 38) sts rem.

Work fully-fashioned decreases each side every fourth row 0 (0, 0, 2, 4) times, every other row 9 (9, 11, 11, 7) times, then every row 6 (8, 4, 0, 0) times—14 (14, 14, 16, 16) sts rem.

BO 2 sts at beg of next four rows.

BO rem 6 (6, 6, 8, 8) sts.

FINISHING
Sew shoulder seams.

Neckband
With RS facing and circular needle, beg at lower right front edge, and pick up and knit 210 sts along right front edge, around back of neck, and down left front edge.

Beg with Row 2 of patt, work even in K2 P2 Rib Patt until band measures approx ¾" from beg. Place markers for four evenly spaced buttonholes along right front edge.

Next Row: Make buttonholes by binding off 2 sts where marked.

Next Row: CO 2 sts over bound-off sts from previous row. Cont even in rib until bands measure approx 1½" from beg.

BO *loosely* in rib.

Set in sleeves.

Sew sleeve and side seams.

Sew buttons opposite buttonholes.

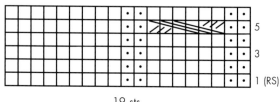

SIMPLE RIGHT CABLE PANEL

5

3

1 (RS)

19 sts

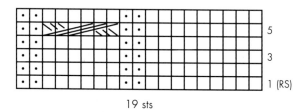

SIMPLE LEFT CABLE PANEL

5

3

1 (RS)

19 sts

KEY

☐ = K on RS; P on WS

• = P on RS; K on WS

 = Slip next 3 sts onto cn and hold in back; K3; K3 from cn

= Slip next 3 sts onto cn and hold in front; K3; K3 from cn

MEANDERING LEFT CABLE PANEL

MEANDERING RIGHT CABLE PANEL

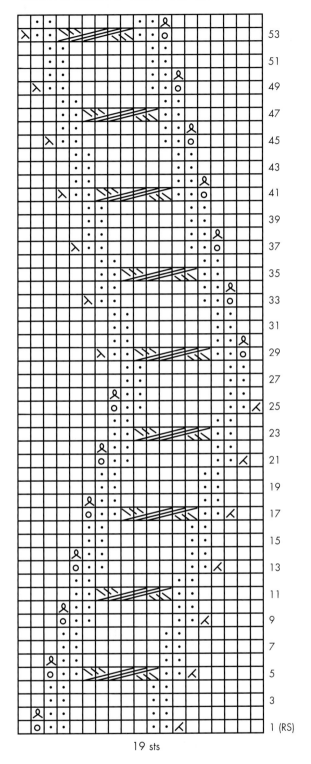

19 sts

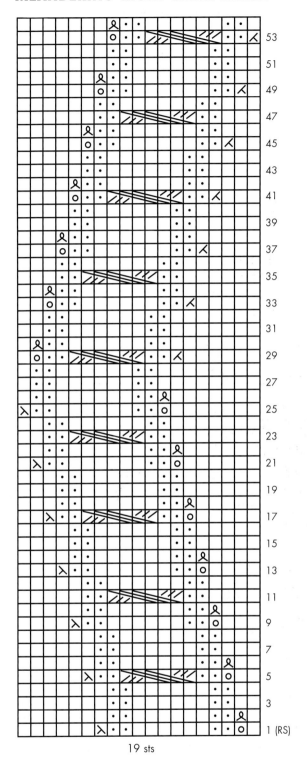

19 sts

KEY

☐ = K on RS; P on WS

• = P on RS; K on WS

Ꝅ = P through back loop

 = Slip next 3 sts onto cn and hold in back; K3; K3 sts from cn

= Slip next 3 sts onto cn and hold in front; K3; K3 sts from cn

o = yarn over

⟋ = K2tog

⟍ = SSK = Slip next 2 sts knitwise one at a time, then insert LH needle into the fronts of these 2 sts and knit them tog from this position

Marissa

A perfect introduction to lace knitting: a fresh burst of color to energize your springtime knitting (and your warm weather wardrobe!). This sweet, short-sleeved top has simple details, allowing you to concentrate on the lovely diamond lace panel that's front and center.

GAUGE

In Stockinette St Patt with larger needles, 22 sts and 32 rows = 4". *To save time, take time to check gauge.*

BORDER PATTERN

(over mult. 2 + 1 sts)

Row 1 (RS): Knit across.

Rows 2-5: As Row 1.

Row 6: *P2tog, yarn over. Repeat from * across, ending row with P1.

Rows 7-12: As Row 1.

STOCKINETTE STITCH PATTERN

(over any number of sts)

Row 1 (RS): Knit across.

Row 2: Purl across.

Repeat Rows 1 and 2 for patt.

DIAMOND LACE PANEL

(over middle 19 sts)

See chart on page 45.

NOTES

SSK = Slip next 2 sts knitwise one at a time, then insert LH needle into the fronts of these 2 sts and knit them tog from this position.

M1 = Insert LH needle under the horizontal thread that is between st just worked and the next st, and knit into the back of it.

For fully-fashioned increases: K2, M1, work across until 2 sts rem in row, ending row with M1, K2.

For fully-fashioned decreases:
on RS rows: K2, SSK, work across in patts as established until 4 sts rem in row, ending row with K2tog, K2;
on WS rows: P2, P2tog, work across in patts as established until 4 sts rem, ending row with P2tog *through their back loops*, P2.

For sweater assembly, refer to the illustration for set-in construction on page 126.

BACK

With smaller needles, CO 81 (89, 99, 109, 119) sts. Work Rows 1-12 of Border Patt, inc 6 (10, 10, 12, 12) sts evenly across last row—87 (99, 109, 121, 131) sts.

Next Row (RS): Change to larger needles, work Row 1 of Stockinette St Patt over first 34 (40, 45, 51, 56) sts, place marker, work Row 1 of Diamond Lace Panel over middle 19 sts, place marker, work Row 1 of Stockinette St Patt to end row.

SKILL LEVEL

Intermediate

SIZES

Small (Medium, Large, Extra-Large, Extra-Extra Large). *Instructions are for smallest size, with changes for other sizes noted in parentheses as necessary.*

FINISHED MEASUREMENTS

Bust: 36 (40, 44, 48, 52)"
Total length: 22"

MATERIALS

Classic Elite's *Provence* (sport weight; 100% mercerized cotton; each approx 4½ oz/ 125 g and 256 yd/233 m), 4 (4, 5, 6, 6) hanks Watermelon #2695

One pair each of sizes 4 and 5 (3.5 and 3.75 mm) knitting needles or size needed to obtain gauge

Cont patts as established, and work fully-fashioned increases each side on eleventh row, and then every twelfth row 0 (0, 0, 0, 1) time, every fourteenth row 1 (0, 5, 0, 4) times, every sixteenth row 4 (0, 0, 2, 0) times, then every eighteenth row 0 (4, 0, 2, 0) times—99 (109, 121, 131, 143) sts.

Work even in patts as established until piece measures approx 14 (13½, 13, 13, 12½)" from beg, ending after WS row.

Shape Armholes

BO 3 (4, 5, 5, 6) sts at beg of next two rows.

BO 2 (2, 3, 3, 3) sts at beg of next two rows—89 (97, 105, 115, 125) sts rem.

Work fully-fashioned decreases each side every row 0 (4, 8, 17, 22) times, then every other row 9 (8, 6, 2, 0) times—71 (73, 77, 77, 81) sts rem.

Cont patts as established until piece measures approx 20½" from beg, ending after WS row.

Shape Neck
Next Row (RS): Work across first 16 (17, 19, 19, 21) sts; join second ball of yarn and BO middle 39 sts, work to end row.

Work both sides at once with separate balls of yarn, and dec 1 st each neck edge every row twice—14 (15, 17, 17, 19) sts rem each side.

Cont even in patts as established until piece measures approx 21" from beg, ending after WS row.

Shape Shoulders
BO 3 (4, 4, 4, 5) sts each shoulder edge three times, then BO 5 (3, 5, 5, 4) sts each shoulder edge once.

FRONT
Same as back until piece measures approx 18" from beg, ending after WS row.

8"

1½"

2½"

1"

7 (7½, 8, 8½)"

FRONT AND BACK

14 (13½, 13, 13, 12½)"

18 (20, 22, 24, 26)"

16 (18, 20, 22, 24)"

11½ (12, 13, 13, 13¼)"

4½ (5, 5½, 5½, 6)"

4"

SLEEVE

9½ (10, 10¾, 10¾, 11)"

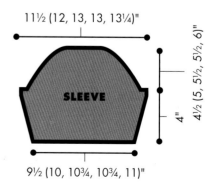

Shape Neck

Next Row (RS): Work across first 25 (26, 28, 28, 30) sts; join second ball of yarn and BO middle 21 sts, work to end row.

Work both sides at once with separate balls of yarn and BO 2 sts each neck edge twice—21 (22, 24, 24, 26) sts rem each side.

Dec 1 st at each neck edge every row twice, then every other row five times—14 (15, 17, 17, 19) sts rem each side.

Cont even until piece measures same as back to shoulders.

Complete same as back.

SLEEVES

With smaller needles, CO 49 (51, 53, 53, 55) sts. Work Rows 1-12 of Border Patt, inc 4 (4, 6, 6, 6) sts evenly across last row—53 (55, 59, 59, 61) sts.

Change to larger needles, beg Stockinette St Patt, and work fully-fashioned increases each side every other row 4 (4, 6, 6, 6) times, then every fourth row 1 (1, 0, 0, 0) times—63 (65, 71, 71, 73) sts.

Cont even until piece measures approx 4" from beg, ending after WS row.

Shape Cap

BO 3 (4, 5, 5, 6) sts at beg of next two rows—57 (57, 61, 61, 61) sts rem.

Work fully-fashioned decreases each side every other row 7 (5, 7, 7, 5) times, then every fourth row 4 (6, 6, 6, 8) times—35 sts rem.

BO 3 sts at beg of next four rows—23 sts rem.

BO.

FINISHING

Sew left shoulder seam.

Neckband

With RS facing and smaller needles, pick up and knit 135 sts around neckline. Work Rows 2-5 of Border Patt, dec 14 sts evenly across last row—121 sts rem. Work Rows 6-10 of Border Patt, dec 14 sts evenly across last row—107 sts rem. Work Rows 11 and 12 of Border Patt.

BO.

Sew right shoulder seam, including side of neckband.

Set in sleeves.

Sew sleeve and side seams.

DIAMOND LACE PANEL

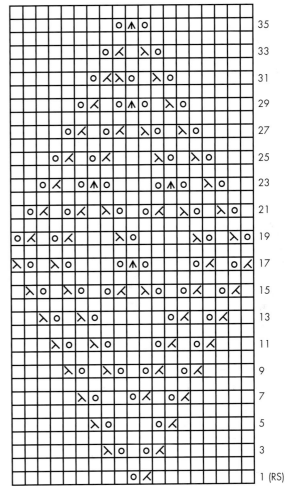

Middle 19 sts

KEY

☐ = K on RS; P on WS

⟋ = K2tog

O = Yarn over

⟍ = SSK

⋀ = Slip next 2 sts at once knitwise; K next st; pass 2 slipped sts over knitted st

Katherine *Knit yourself a knockout!*

Simple, supple ribs gracefully intertwine in a beautiful cable medallion. When they diverge for the neck opening, they draw the eye upward and create an elegant self-finished trim.

GAUGE

In Ribbed Patt, *unstretched*, 42 sts and 31 rows = 4". **To save time, take time to check gauge.**

K2 P2 RIB PATTERN

(over mult. 4 + 2 sts)

Row 1 (RS): *K2, P2. Repeat from * across, ending row with K2.

Row 2: *P2, K2. Repeat from * across, ending row with P2.

Repeat Rows 1 and 2 for patt.

DIAMOND CABLE PANEL

(54 sts increases to 56 sts)
See chart on page 49.

NOTES

M1 = Insert LH needle under the horizontal thread that is between st just worked and the next st, and knit into the back of it.

SSK = Slip next 2 sts knitwise one at a time, then insert LH needle into the fronts of these 2 sts and knit them tog from this position.

BACK

CO 170 (186, 202, 218) sts. Beg K2 P2 Rib Patt, and work even until piece measures approx 35½" from beg, ending after WS row.

Beg Cable Panel

Next Row (RS): Work rib as established across first 58 (66, 74, 82) sts, place marker, work Row 1 of Diamond Cable Panel over middle 54 sts, place marker, work rib as established to end row— 171 (187, 203, 219) sts.

Cont patts as established until Row 54 of Diamond Cable Panel is completed— 172 (188, 204, 220) sts.

Shape Neck and Armholes

Next Row (RS): K2, P2, K1, SSK, P1, (K2, P2) 17 (19, 21, 23) times, K2, P1, K2tog, K1, P2, K2; join second ball of yarn and K2, P2, K1, SSK, work rib as established until 7 sts rem in row, ending row with K2tog, K1, P2, K2.

Next Row: P2, K2, P1, P2tog, work rib as established until 7 sts rem on first side, P2tog *through back loops*, P1, K2, P2; on second side of neck, P2, K2, P1, P2tog, work rib as established until 7 sts rem in row, ending row with P2tog *through back loops*, P1, K2, P2.

SKILL LEVEL
Advanced

SIZES
Small (Medium, Large, Extra-Large). *Instructions are for smallest size, with changes for other sizes noted in parentheses as necessary.*

FINISHED MEASUREMENTS
Bust: 32 (35½, 38½, 42)"
Total length: 49½ (49½, 50, 50)"

MATERIALS
Muench Yarns/GGH Yarns's *Maxima* (sport weight; 100% merino wool; each approx 1¾ oz/50 g and 120 yd/110 m), 22 (24, 26, 28) balls Brick #18

One pair of size 5 (3.75 mm) knitting needles or size needed to obtain gauge

Cable needle

Stitch markers

HOT TIP

Getting an accurate gauge measurement in ribbed fabrics can be tricky. For best results, be sure to take all measurements with your fabric completely unstretched, staying away from the selvage stitches as well as the cast-on and bound-off edges. And don't forget to count the stitches hidden in those purl "valleys"!

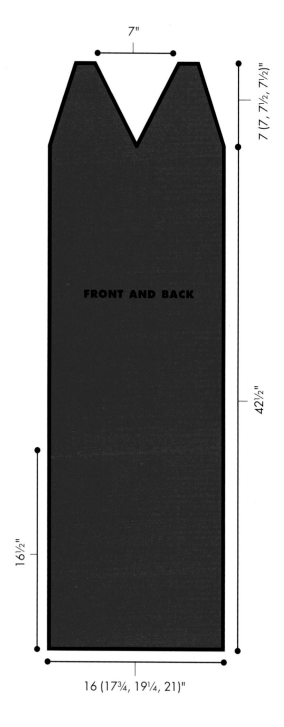

FRONT AND BACK

7"

7 (7, 7½, 7½)"

42½"

16½"

16 (17¾, 19¼, 21)"

Cont working fully-fashioned decreases 7 sts before or after each neck edge every row 24 (24, 20, 20) more times, then every other row 10 (10, 14, 14) times; and at the same time, work fully-fashioned decreases 7 sts before or after each armhole edge every row 16 (32, 44, 54) more times, then every other row 14 (6, 2, 0) times—18 sts rem each side.

Work even until armholes measure approx 7 (7, 7½, 7½)" from beg.

BO.

FRONT

Same as back.

FINISHING

Sew shoulder seams.

Sew side seams, leaving 16½" open at lower right side seam for side slit.

DIAMOND CABLE PANEL

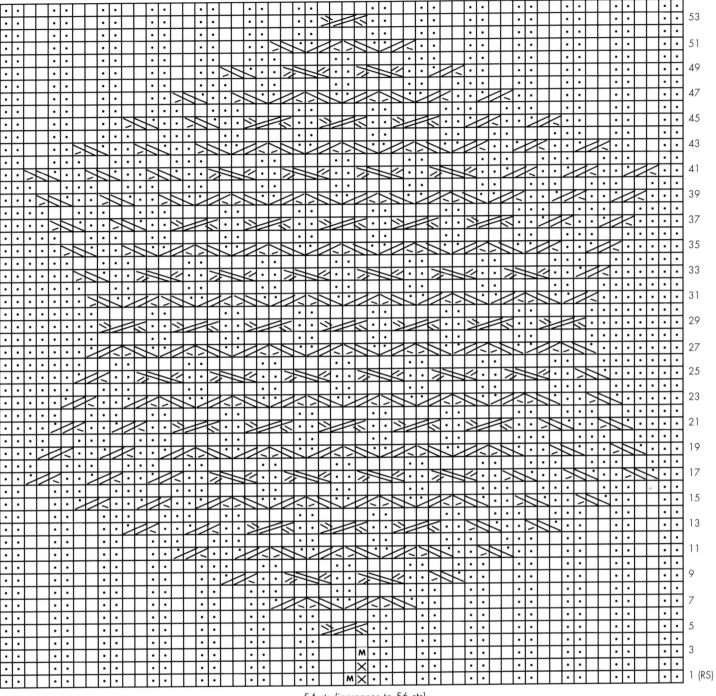

54 sts (increases to 56 sts)

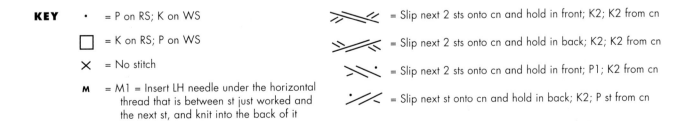

KEY

• = P on RS; K on WS

☐ = K on RS; P on WS

✕ = No stitch

M = M1 = Insert LH needle under the horizontal thread that is between st just worked and the next st, and knit into the back of it

= Slip next 2 sts onto cn and hold in front; K2; K2 from cn

= Slip next 2 sts onto cn and hold in back; K2; K2 from cn

= Slip next 2 sts onto cn and hold in front; P1; K2 from cn

= Slip next st onto cn and hold in back; K2; P st from cn

Erin

An unexpected color palette puts a hot spin on this traditional winter warmer. Its color-blocking is a great figure-flattering device: Those light, bright colors draw the eye upward!

GAUGE
In Stockinette St Patt with larger needles, 20 sts and 26 rows = 4". **To save time, take time to check gauge.**

K1 P1 RIB PATTERN
(over mult. 2 + 1 sts)

Row 1 (RS): *K1, P1. Repeat from * across, ending row with K1.

Row 2: *P1, K1. Repeat from * across, ending row with P1.

Repeat Rows 1 and 2 for patt.

STOCKINETTE STITCH PATTERN
(over any number of sts)

Row 1 (RS): Knit across.

Row 2: Purl across.

Repeat Rows 1 and 2 for patt.

FAIR ISLE PATTERN
See charts on page 53.

NOTES
For fully-fashioned decreases:
on RS rows: K1, SSK, work across in patt as established until 3 sts rem in row, ending row with K2tog, K1;
on WS rows: P1, P2tog, work across in patt as established until 3 sts rem in row, ending row with P2tog *through their back loops*, P1.

SSK = Slip next 2 sts knitwise one at a time, then insert LH needle into the fronts of these 2 sts and knit them tog from this position.

For sweater assembly, refer to the illustration for set-in construction on page 126.

BACK
With smaller needles and A, CO 91 (97, 103, 115, 121) sts. Change to B, and work even in K1 P1 Rib Patt until piece measures approx 2½" from beg, ending after WS row.

Change to larger needles, beg Stockinette St Patt, and work even with B until piece measures approx 9¾ (10, 10, 10, 10)" from beg, ending after WS row.

Beg Fair Isle Patt Row 1 where indicated on chart, and work even until piece measures approx 13½ (13¾, 14, 14, 14)" from beg, ending after WS row.

Shape Armholes
Cont Fair Isle Patt as established, BO 3 (3, 4, 4, 5) sts at beg of next two rows, then BO 2 (2, 2, 3, 3) sts at beg of next two rows—81 (87, 91, 101, 105) sts rem.

Dec 1 st each side every row 1 (6, 6, 15, 16) times, then every other row 6 (4, 5, 1, 1) times—67 (67, 69, 69, 71) sts rem.

When Row 48 of Fair Isle Patt is completed, cont even with F until piece measures approx 21 (21½, 22, 22½, 23)" from beg, ending after WS row.

Shape Shoulders
BO 4 sts each shoulder edge three times, then BO 4 (4, 5, 5, 6) sts each shoulder edge once.

BO rem 35 sts for back of neck.

FRONT
Same as back until piece measures approx 19½ (20, 20½, 21, 21½)" from beg, ending after WS row.

Shape Neck
Next Row (RS): Work across first 26 (26, 27, 27, 28) sts; join second ball of yarn and BO middle 15 sts, cont patt as established to end row.

SKILL LEVEL
Intermediate

SIZES
Extra-Small (Small, Medium, Large, Extra-Large).
Instructions are for smallest size, with changes for other sizes noted in parentheses as necessary.

FINISHED MEASUREMENTS
Bust: 36½ (39, 41½, 46, 48½)"
Total length: 22 (22½, 23, 23½, 24)"

MATERIALS
Aurora Yarn/Garnstudio's *Karisma* (light worsted weight; 100% superwash wool; each approx 1¾ oz/ 50 g and 121 yd/110 m), 2 (2, 3, 3, 4) balls Purple #38 (A), 5 (5, 6, 6, 7) balls Dark Green #47 (B), 2 (2, 2, 3, 3) balls Orange #11 (C), 3 (3, 3, 4, 4) balls Gold #10 (D), 1 (2, 2, 2, 2) balls Scarlet #18 (E), and 5 (5, 6, 6, 7) balls Light Green #45 (F)

One pair each of sizes 6 and 7 (4 and 4.5 mm) knitting needles or size needed to obtain gauge

Work both sides at once with separate balls of yarn, and BO 3 sts each neck edge twice—20 (20, 21, 21, 22) sts rem each side.

Dec 1 st each neck edge every row three times, then every other row once—16 (16, 17, 17, 18) sts rem each side.

Cont even, if necessary, until piece measures same as back to shoulders, ending after WS row.

Shape Shoulders
Same as back.

SLEEVES

With smaller needles and A, CO 43 sts. Change to B, and work K1 P1 Rib Patt until piece measures approx 2½" from beg, ending after WS row.

Change to larger needles, and beg Fair Isle Patt where indicated on chart, and work even for two rows.

Cont patt as established, inc 1 st each side every fourth row 3 (6, 8, 14, 20) times, then every sixth row 12 (10, 9, 5, 1) times, working in F after Row 48 of Fair Isle Patt is completed—73 (75, 77, 81, 85) sts.

Cont even until piece measures approx 18 (18, 18½, 18½, 18½)" from beg, ending after WS row.

Shape Cap
BO 3 (3, 4, 4, 5) sts at beg of next two rows—67 (69, 69, 73, 75) sts rem.

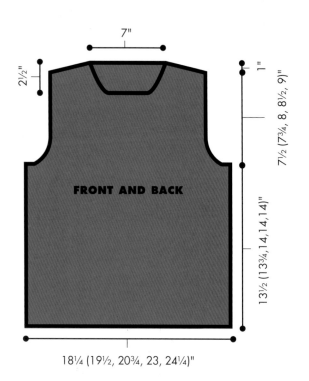

FRONT AND BACK

7"

2½"

1"

7½ (7¾, 8, 8½, 9)"

13½ (13¾, 14, 14, 14)"

18¼ (19½, 20¾, 23, 24¼)"

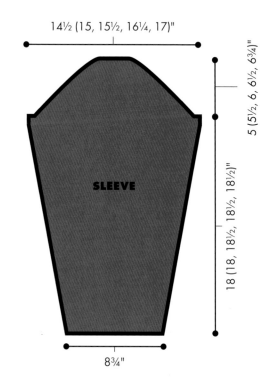

SLEEVE

14½ (15, 15½, 16¼, 17)"

5 (5½, 6, 6½, 6¾)"

18 (18, 18½, 18½, 18½)"

8¾"

Work fully-fashioned decreases each side every other row 3 (5, 8, 10, 10) times, then every row 20 (19, 16, 16, 17) times—21 sts rem.

BO 2 sts at beg of next four rows—13 sts rem.

BO.

FINISHING
Sew left shoulder seam.

Neckband
With RS facing, smaller needles, and F, pick up and knit 82 sts around neckline. Work K1 P1 Rib Patt until band measures approx 3½" from beg.

Change to A, and work one more row of rib.

BO *loosely* in rib.

Sew right shoulder seam, including side of neckband.

Set in sleeves. Sew sleeve and side seams.

HOT TIP

Frustrated by tangled yarns when knitting Fair Isle patterns? Minimize the mess by alternating between picking up one color from beneath the other and one color from above the other all the way across each row. You'll knit faster—and feel happier. Try it!

FAIR ISLE PATTERN, ROWS 1-37

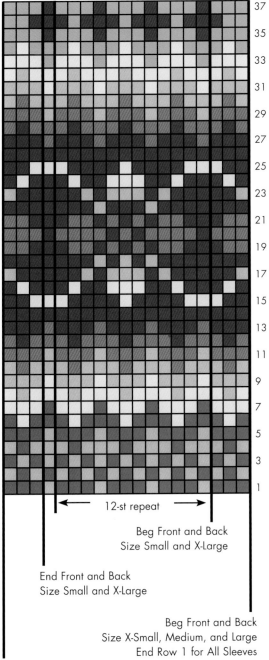

37
35
33
31
29
27
25
23
21
19
17
15
13
11
9
7
5
3
1

← 12-st repeat →

Beg Front and Back
Size Small and X-Large

End Front and Back
Size Small and X-Large

Beg Front and Back
Size X-Small, Medium, and Large
End Row 1 for All Sleeves

End Front and Back
Size X-Small, Medium, and Large
End Row 1 for All Sleeves

FAIR ISLE PATTERN, ROWS 38-48

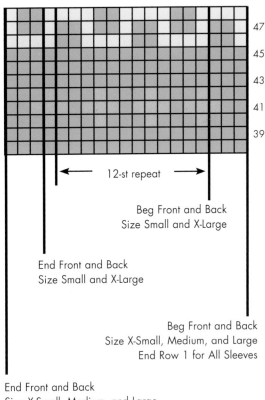

47
45
43
41
39

← 12-st repeat →

Beg Front and Back
Size Small and X-Large

End Front and Back
Size Small and X-Large

Beg Front and Back
Size X-Small, Medium, and Large
End Row 1 for All Sleeves

End Front and Back
Size X-Small, Medium, and Large
End Row 1 for All Sleeves

KEY

■ = A		▫ = D	
■ = B		▨ = E	
■ = C		▨ = F	

Joy

Fun and flirty, this super-soft and swingy top is as light as a feather. Don't be intimidated by the large number of stitches in the cast-on row. They become fewer and fewer as you go!

GAUGE

In Rib Patt #2, 32 sts and 30 rows = 4".
To save time, take time to check gauge.

RIB PATTERN #1

(over mult. 13 + 2 sts)

Row 1 (RS): P3, *K9, P4. Repeat from * across, ending row with K9, P3.

Row 2: K3, *P9, K4. Repeat from * across, ending row with P9, K3.

Repeat Rows 1 and 2 for patt.

RIB PATTERN #2

(over mult. 7 + 2 sts)

Row 1 (RS): P3, *K3, P4. Repeat from * across, ending row with K3, P3.

Row 2: K3, *P3, K4. Repeat from * across, ending row with P3, K3.

Repeat Rows 1 and 2 for patt.

NOTES

Throughout, instructions include one selvage st each side; these sts are not reflected in final measurements.

SSK = Slip next 2 sts knitwise one at a time, then insert LH needle into the fronts of these 2 sts and knit them tog from this position.

SSSK = Slip next 3 sts knitwise one at a time, then insert LH needle into the fronts of these 3 sts and knit them tog from this position.

When decreasing, Raglan Dec Row 1 eliminates 2 sts on each side of fabric; Raglan Dec Row 2 eliminates 1 st on each side of fabric.

M1 = Insert LH needle under the horizontal thread that is between st

just worked and the next st, and knit into the back of it.

For sweater assembly, refer to the illustration for raglan construction on page 126.

BACK

CO 262 (288, 314, 340) sts. Beg Rib Patt #1, working Rows 1 and 2 of patt 10 (10, 9, 9) times total.

Next Row (RS): P3 *K1, SSK, K3, K2tog, K1, P4. Repeat from * across, ending row with K1, SSK, K3, K2tog, K1, P3—222 (244, 266, 288) sts.

Work even, knitting the knit sts and purling the purl sts, for 19 (19, 17, 17) more rows.

Next Row (RS): P3, *K1, SSK, K1, K2tog, K1, P4. Repeat from * across, ending row with K1, SSK, K1, K2tog, K1, P3—182 (200, 218, 236) sts.

Work even, knitting the knit sts and purling the purl sts, for 19 (19, 17, 17) more rows.

Next Row (RS): P3, *SSK, K1, K2tog, P4. Repeat from * across, ending row with SSK, K1, K2tog, P3—142 (156, 170, 184) sts.

SKILL LEVEL
Intermediate

SIZES
Small (Medium, Large, Extra-Large). *Instructions are for smallest size, with changes for other sizes noted in parentheses as necessary.*

FINISHED MEASUREMENTS
Bust: 35 (38½, 42, 45½)"
Total length: 17¼ (17¾, 18¼, 19¼)"

MATERIALS
Muench Yarns/GGH Yarns's *Soft Kid* (sport weight; 70% super kid mohair/ 25% nylon/5% wool; each approx .875 oz/25 g and 154 yd/138 m), 10 (10, 12, 14) balls Fuchsia #28

One pair of size 6 (4 mm) knitting needles or size needed to obtain gauge

Work even, if necessary, knitting the knit sts and purling the purl sts, until piece measures approx 8¾ (8¼, 7¾, 8¼)" from beg, ending after WS row.

Shape Armholes

Raglan Dec Row 1 (RS): P3, K2, SSSK, knit the knit sts and purl the purl sts until 8 sts rem in row, ending row with K3tog, K2, P3.

Next Row: Knit the knit sts and purl the purl sts.

Raglan Dec Row 2: P3, K2, SSK, knit the knit sts and purl the purl sts until 7 sts rem in row, ending row with K2tog, K2, P3.

Next Row: Knit the knit sts and purl the purl sts.

Repeat last four rows 6 (7, 8, 5) more times—100 (108, 116, 148) sts.

Work Raglan Dec Row 1 on RS rows 14 (16, 18, 26) times, knitting the knit sts and purling the purl sts on all WS rows—44 sts.

BO in rib.

FRONT

Same as back.

SLEEVES

CO 58 (58, 72, 86) sts. Beg Rib Patt #2, and work even for ½", ending after WS row.

Inc Row (RS): P3, K3, M1, cont patt as established until 6 sts rem in row, ending row with M1, K3, P3.

Cont patt as established, and work Inc Row every fourth row 2 (25, 27, 6) more times, then every sixth row 18 (2, 0, 14) times, working new sts into Rib Patt #2—100 (114, 128, 128) sts.

Cont even until piece measures approx 17 (17½, 17, 17)" from beg, ending after WS row.

Shape Cap

Raglan Dec Row 1 (RS): P3, K2, SSSK, knit the knit sts and purl the purl sts until 8 sts rem in row, ending row with K3tog, K2, P3.

Next Row: Knit the knit sts and purl the purl sts.

Raglan Dec Row 2: P3, K2, SSK, knit the knit sts and purl the purl sts until 7 sts rem in row, ending row with K2tog, K2, P3.

Next Row: Knit the knit sts and purl the purl sts.

Repeat last four rows 13 (14, 15, 17) more times—16 (24, 32, 20) sts.

Work Raglan Dec Row 1 on RS rows 0 (2, 4, 1) times, knitting the knit sts and purling the purl sts on all WS rows—16 sts.

For Size Extra-Large Only:
Work two rows even.

For All Sizes:
BO in rib.

FINISHING

Sew raglan seams.

Sew sleeve and side seams.

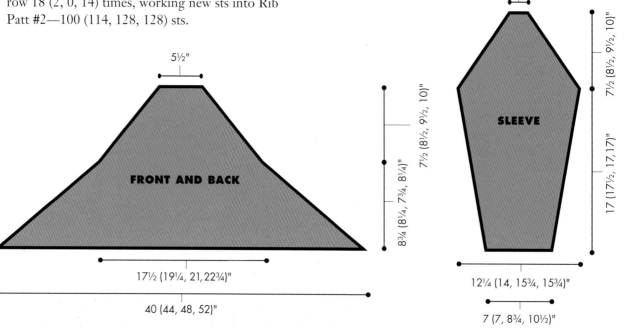

FRONT AND BACK

5½"

17½ (19¼, 21, 22¾)"

40 (44, 48, 52)"

8¾ (8¼, 7¾, 8¼)"

1¾"

SLEEVE

7½ (8½, 9½, 10)"

17 (17½, 17, 17)"

7½ (8½, 9½, 10)"

12¼ (14, 15¾, 15¾)"

7 (7, 8¾, 10½)"

Deborah

Whip up this jacket in no time, and let the yarn do all the work! This design, worked in a multicolored and textured yarn, is as easy to knit as it is to wear.

GAUGE

In Stockinette St Patt with larger needles, 10 sts and 15 rows = 4". *To save time, take time to check gauge.*

GARTER STITCH PATTERN

(over any number of sts)
Patt Row: Knit across.

Repeat Patt Row.

STOCKINETTE STITCH PATTERN

(over any number of sts)
Row 1 (RS): Knit across.

Row 2: Purl across.

Repeat Rows 1 and 2 for patt.

NOTES

Throughout, instructions include one selvage st each side; these sts are not reflected in final measurements.

For ease in finishing, seams may be sewn using a smooth yarn rather than the main knitting yarn; be sure to choose one with similar laundering instructions.

For sweater assembly, refer to the illustration for square indented construction on page 126.

BACK

With smaller needles, CO 47 (51, 54, 60, 65) sts. Work Garter St Patt until piece measures approx 3" from beg, inc 5 (5, 6, 6, 7) sts evenly across last row— 52 (56, 60, 66, 72) sts.

Change to larger needles, and beg Stockinette St Patt.

Cont even until piece measures approx 22 (22½, 22½, 22½, 22½)" from beg, ending after WS row.

Shape Armholes

BO 9 (10, 11, 12, 13) sts at beg of next two rows—34 (36, 38, 42, 46) sts rem.

Cont even in patt as established until piece measures approx 30½ (31½, 32, 32, 32½)" from beg, ending after WS row.

Shape Shoulders

BO 3 (3, 4, 4, 5) sts at beg of next four rows. BO 3 (4, 3, 5, 5) sts at beg of next two rows.

BO rem 16 sts.

LEFT FRONT

With smaller needles, CO 16 (18, 20, 22, 25) sts. Work Garter St Patt until piece measures approx 3" from beg,

SKILL LEVEL
Advanced Beginner

SIZES
Small (Medium, Large, Extra-Large, Extra-Extra Large). *Instructions are for smallest size, with changes for other sizes noted in parentheses as necessary.*

FINISHED MEASUREMENTS
Bust: 40 (43½, 46½, 51½, 56)"

Total length: 32 (33, 33½, 33½, 34)"

MATERIALS
JCA/Artful Yarn's *Circus* (bulky weight; 95% wool/ 5% acrylic; each approx 3½ oz/100 g and 93 yd/ 85 m), 10 (11, 12, 13, 14) balls Tightrope Walker #8

One pair each of sizes 10 and 11 (6 and 8 mm) knitting needles or size needed to obtain gauge

36" Circular knitting needle, size 10 (6 mm)

HOT TIP

For a totally different look, consider making the collar, front bands, and lower 6 inches of sleeves with a contrasting yarn. Just make sure its laundering instructions and knitting gauge match those of the original!

inc 2 (2, 2, 3, 3) sts evenly across last row—18 (20, 22, 25, 28) sts.

Change to larger needles, and beg Stockinette St Patt.

Work even until piece measures approx 22 (22½, 22½, 22½, 22½)" from beg, ending after WS row.

Shape Armhole

BO 9 (10, 11, 12, 13) sts at beg of next row—9 (10, 11, 13, 15) sts rem.

Cont even in patt as established until piece measures approx 30½ (31½, 32, 32, 32½)" from beg, ending after WS row.

Shape Shoulder

BO 3 (3, 4, 4, 5) sts at shoulder edge twice. Work one row even.

BO rem 3 (4, 3, 5, 5) sts.

RIGHT FRONT

Same as left front *except* reverse all shaping.

SLEEVES

With smaller needles, CO 24 (25, 25, 25, 27) sts. Work Garter St Patt until piece measures approx 6" from beg, inc 2 (3, 3, 3, 3) sts evenly across last row—26 (28, 28, 28, 30) sts.

Change to larger needles, beg Stockinette St Patt, and inc 1 st each side every other row 0 (0, 0, 0, 2) times, then every fourth row 2 (2, 9, 11, 9) times, then every sixth row 7 (7, 2, 0, 0) times—44 (46, 50, 50, 52) sts.

Cont even until piece measures approx 24 (24¼, 24½, 23½, 22¾)" from beg, ending after WS row.

BO.

FINISHING

Sew shoulder seams.

Collar and Front Bands

With RS facing and circular needle, beg at lower right front edge and pick up and knit 79 (82, 84, 84, 86) sts evenly along right front edge, 15 sts along back of neck, and 79 (82, 84, 84, 86) sts along left front edge—173 (179, 183, 183, 187) sts total. Work rows of Garter St Patt, increasing one st at center back of neck every sixth row three times—176 (182, 186, 186, 190) sts.

Cont even until band measures approx 6" from beg.

BO.

Set in sleeves.

Sew side and sleeve seams, sewing lower 3" of sleeve seams on the RS, since the cuff will be folded back.

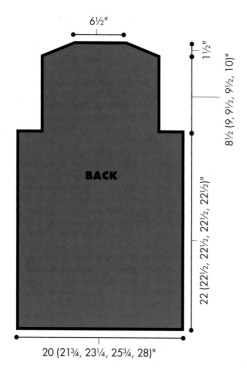

6½"
1½"
8½ (9, 9½, 9½, 10)"
BACK
22 (22½, 22½, 22½, 22½)"
20 (21¾, 23¼, 25¾, 28)"
1½"
8½ (9, 9½, 9½, 10)"
LEFT FRONT
22 (22½, 22½, 22½, 22½)"
6½ (7¼, 8, 9¼, 10½)"
17 (17½, 19¼, 19¼, 20)"
SLEEVE
24 (24¼, 24½, 23½, 22¾)"
9½ (10½, 10½, 10½, 11¼)"

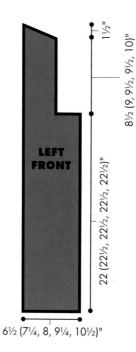

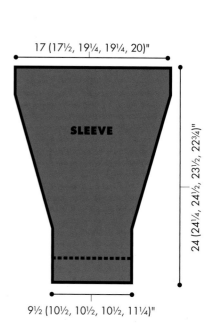

Diana

This sweater sizzles! Worked in lustrous mercerized cotton, its twisted vertical ribs accentuate all the right curves.

GAUGE

In Stockinette St Patt, 22 sts and 29 rows = 4". **To save time, take time to check gauge.**

STOCKINETTE STITCH PATTERN

(over any number of sts)

Row 1 (RS): Knit across.

Row 2: Purl across.

Repeat Rows 1 and 2 for patt.

BORDER TWISTED RIB PATTERN

(over mult. 3 + 2 sts)

Row 1 (RS): P2, *K next st *through the back loop only*, P2. Repeat from * across.

Row 2: K2, *P next st *through the back loop only*, K2. Repeat from * across.

Repeat Rows 1 and 2 for patt.

CENTER TWISTED RIB PATTERN

(over middle 26 sts)

Row 1 (RS): P2, *K next st *through the back loop only*, P2. Repeat from * seven more times.

Row 2: K2, *P next st *through the back loop only*, K2. Repeat from * seven more times.

Repeat Rows 1 and 2 for patt.

SIDE RIB PATTERN

(over 14 sts)

Row 1 (RS): P2, *K next st *through the back loop only*, P2. Repeat from * three more times.

Row 2: K2, *P next st *through the back loop only*, K2. Repeat from * three more times.

Repeat Rows 1 and 2 for patt.

NOTES

SSK = Slip next 2 sts knitwise one at a time, then insert LH needle into the fronts of these 2 sts and knit them tog from this position.

M1 = Insert LH needle under the horizontal thread that is between st just worked and the next st, and knit into the back of it.

For Body Dec Row: on RS rows: Work Row 1 of Side Rib Patt over first 14 sts, slip marker, SSK, work in patt as established until 16 sts rem in row, ending row with K2tog, slip marker, work Row 1 of Side Rib Patt over last 14 sts; *on WS rows:* Work Row 2 of Side Rib Patt over first 14 sts, slip marker, P2tog, work in patt as established until 16 sts rem in row, ending row with P2tog *through their back loops*, slip marker, work Row 2 of Side Rib Patt over last 14 sts.

For Front Neck Dec Row (RS rows only): Work across first side of front until 14 sts rem this side of neck, K2tog, (P2, K next st *through back loop only*) four times, P1; on second side of neck, with second ball of yarn, P1, (K next st *through back loop only*, P2) four times, SSK, work across to end row.

SKILL LEVEL

Intermediate

SIZES

Extra-Small (Small, Medium, Large, Extra-Large). *Instructions are for smallest size, with changes for other sizes noted in parentheses as necessary.*

FINISHED MEASUREMENTS

Bust: 32 (34, 36½, 39, 41)"

Total length: 22 (22½, 23, 23½, 23½)"

MATERIALS

Aurora Yarns/Garnstudio's *Muskat* (light worsted weight; 100% Egyptian mercerized cotton; each approx 1¾ oz/ 50 g and 109 yd/100 m), 8 (9, 10, 11, 12) balls Honeysuckle #51

One pair of size 5 (3.75 mm) knitting needles or size needed to obtain gauge

Stitch markers

BACK

CO 104 (110, 116, 122, 128) sts. Beg Border Twisted Rib Patt, and work even until piece measures approx 1¼" from beg, ending after WS row.

Next Row (RS): Work Row 1 of Side Rib Patt over first 14 sts, place marker, K25 (28, 31, 34, 37) sts, place marker, work Row 1 of Center Twisted Rib Patt over next 26 sts, place marker, K25 (28, 31, 34, 37) sts, place marker, work Row 1 of Side Rib Patt over 14 sts to end row.

Next Row (WS): Work Row 2 of Side Rib Patt over first 14 sts, slip marker, P25 (28, 31, 34, 37) sts, slip marker, work Row 2 of Center Twisted Rib Patt over next 26 sts, slip marker, P25 (28, 31, 34, 37) sts, slip marker, work Row 2 of Side Rib Patt over 14 sts to end row.

Repeat last two rows until piece measures approx 3" from beg, ending after WS row.

Waist Shaping

Next Row (RS): Work Body Dec Row.

Cont patts as established, and repeat Body Dec Row every sixth row four more times—94 (100, 106, 112, 118) sts.

Work even until piece measures approx 9½ (9¾, 9¾, 9¾, 9¾)" from beg, ending after WS row.

Inc Row (RS): Work Row 1 of Side Rib Patt over first 14 sts, slip marker, M1, work patts as established to second marker, ending row with remove marker, M1, replace marker, work Row 1 of Side Rib Patt over last 14 sts.

Cont patts as established, and repeat Inc Row every sixth row four more times—104 (110, 116, 122, 128) sts.

Work even until piece measures approx 14" from beg, ending after WS row.

Shape Armholes

Next Row (RS): Work Body Dec Row.

Cont patts as established, and repeat Body Dec Row every other row 11 (11, 13, 11, 10) times, then every row 0 (2, 2, 6, 10) times—80 (82, 84, 86, 86) sts.

Cont even in patts as established until piece measures approx 20 (20½, 21, 21½, 21½)" from beg, ending after WS row.

Shape Neck

Next Row (RS): Work patt as established across first

10 sts; join second ball of yarn and BO middle 60 (62, 64, 66, 66) sts, work patt as established to end row.

Work both sides at once with separate balls of yarn and dec 1 st each neck edge every other row once—9 sts rem each side.

Work even until piece measures approx 21 (21½, 22, 22½, 22½)" from beg, ending after WS row.

Shape Shoulders

BO 2 sts each shoulder edge three times. BO 3 sts each shoulder edge once.

FRONT

Same as back until piece measures approx 15¾ (16¼, 16½, 17, 17)" from beg, ending after WS row. Place marker on knitting needle between the two middle sts as a guide for dividing the neck opening.

Shape Neck

Next Row (RS): Work Row 1 of Side Rib Patt over first 14 sts, slip marker, SSK, work patts as established until 15 sts before center marker, K2tog, (P2, K next st *through back loop only*) four times, P1; for second side of neck, join second ball of yarn, P1, (K next st *through back loop only*, P2) four times, SSK, work patts as established until 16 sts rem in row, ending row with K2tog, slip marker, work Row 1 of Side Rib Patt over last 14 sts.

Work both sides at once with separate balls of yarn, cont armhole shaping same as for back, *and at the same time*, work Front Neck Dec Row every other row 16 (18, 19, 20, 20) times, then every fourth row 1 (0, 0, 0, 0) times—22 sts rem each side.

Cont even, twisting the knit sts that used to be the K2tog or SSK during neck decreases, until piece measures same as back to shoulders, ending after WS row.

Shape Shoulders

Same as for back—13 sts rem each side for neckbands.

Cont even on 13 sts each side until neckbands, when slightly stretched, meet at center back of neck.

BO.

FINISHING

Sew shoulder seams.

Sew sides of neckbands to neckline. Sew bound-off edges of neckbands tog at back of neck.

Sew side seams.

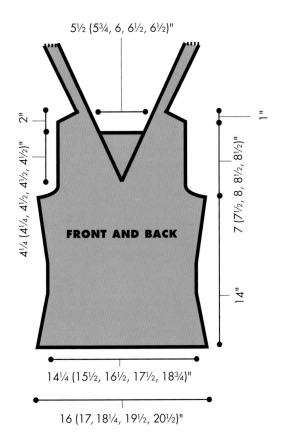

5½ (5¾, 6, 6½, 6½)"

2"

4¼ (4¼, 4½, 4½, 4½)"

1"

7 (7½, 8, 8½, 8½)"

14"

FRONT AND BACK

14¼ (15½, 16½, 17½, 18¾)"

16 (17, 18¼, 19½, 20½)"

Rachel

Sure to become a wardrobe staple, this refined tunic has wonderful knit-in touches: comfortable side slits, a plunging neckline, and a stand-up collar, all worked in noncurling seed stitch.

GAUGE

In Stockinette St Patt, 15 sts and 22 rows = 4". ***To save time, take time to check gauge.***

DOUBLE SEED STITCH PATTERN

(over mult. 2 + 1 sts)

Row 1 (RS): K1, *P1, K1. Repeat from * across.

Row 2: P1, *K1, P1. Repeat from * across.

Row 3: As Row 2.

Row 4: As Row 1.

Repeat Rows 1–4 for patt.

STOCKINETTE STITCH PATTERN

(over any number of sts)

Row 1 (RS): Knit across.

Row 2: Purl across.

Repeat Rows 1 and 2 for patt.

NOTES

Throughout, instructions include one selvage st each side; these sts are not reflected in final measurements.

SSK = Slip next 2 sts knitwise one at a time, then insert LH needle into the fronts of these 2 sts and knit them tog from this position.

For fully-fashioned decreases:
on RS rows: K2, SSK, work across in patt as established until 4 sts rem in row, ending row with K2tog, K2;
on WS rows: P2, P2tog, work across in patt as established until 4 sts rem in row, ending row with P2tog *through their back loops*, P2.

To cast on at the beginning of front neck shaping, do a knit-on cast-on as follows: *Insert RH needle into the first stitch on the LH needle, knit up a stitch and immediately transfer it back to the LH needle. Repeat from * until the required number of stitches is cast on.

For sweater assembly, refer to the illustration for set-in construction on page 126.

BACK

CO 69 (75, 81, 87, 93) sts. Beg Double Seed St Patt, and work even for eight rows.

Next Row (RS): Work Row 1 of Double Seed St Patt over first 5 sts, place marker, work Row 1 of Stockinette St Patt over middle 59 (65, 71, 77, 83) sts, place marker, work Row 1 of Double Seed St Patt to end row.

Work even in patts as established until piece measures approx 6" from beg, ending after WS row.

Next Row (RS): Discontinue Double Seed St Patt, and work Row 1 of

SKILL LEVEL
Advanced

SIZES
Extra-Small (Small, Medium, Large, Extra-Large). *Instructions are for smallest size, with changes for other sizes noted in parentheses as necessary.*

FINISHED MEASUREMENTS
Bust: 36 (39, 42, 45½, 48½)"
Total length: 27 (27, 27, 27½, 28)"

MATERIALS
Rowan/Westminster Fibers's *Cork* (bulky weight; 90% merino wool/10% nylon; each approx 1¾ oz/50 g and 120 yd/110 m), 9 (10, 11, 12, 13) balls Sour #050

One pair of size 10½ (6.5 mm) knitting needles or size needed to obtain gauge

Two stitch holders

Stitch markers

Stockinette St Patt over all 69 (75, 81, 87, 93) sts.

Cont even until piece measures approx 18½" from beg, ending after WS row.

Shape Armholes

BO 2 (2, 4, 5, 6) sts at beg of next two rows—65 (71, 73, 77, 81) sts rem.

Work fully-fashioned decreases each side every row 3 (8, 8, 10, 10) times, then every other row 4 (2, 2, 2, 3) times—51 (51, 53, 53, 55) sts rem.

Cont even until piece measures approx 25½ (25½, 25½, 26, 26½)" from beg, ending after WS row.

Shape Neck

Next Row (RS): K13 (13, 14, 14, 15) sts; join second ball of yarn and BO middle 25 sts, knit across to end row.

Work both sides at once with separate balls of yarn, and dec 1 st each neck edge once—12 (12, 13, 13, 14) sts rem each side.

Cont even until piece measures approx 26 (26, 26, 26½, 27)" from beg, ending after WS row.

6¾"

1" 1½"

1" 1"

8½"

7½ (7½, 7½, 8, 8½)"

FRONT AND BACK

18½"

18 (19½, 21, 22¾, 24¼)"

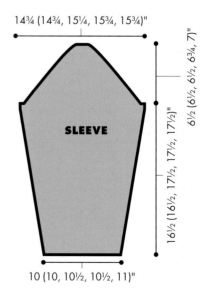

14¾ (14¾, 15¼, 15¾, 15¾)"

6½ (6½, 6½, 6¾, 7)"

SLEEVE

16½ (16½, 17½, 17½, 17½)"

10 (10, 10½, 10½, 11)"

Shape Shoulders

BO 4 sts each shoulder edge twice, then BO 4 (4, 5, 5, 6) sts each shoulder edge once.

FRONT

Same as back until piece measures approx 16 (16, 16, 16½, 17)" from beg, ending after WS row.

Shape Neck

Next Row (RS): Knit across first 30 (33, 36, 39, 42) sts, K2tog, place marker, work Row 1 of Double Seed St Patt over next 5 sts; *with separate ball of yarn,* CO 5 sts, then work Row 1 of Double Seed St Patt over these 5 newly cast-on sts, place marker, SSK, knit across to end row—36 (39, 42, 45, 48) sts each side.

Work even for five rows as follows: Work Stockinette St Patt until first marker, work Double Seed St Patt over next 5 sts; *with second ball of yarn,* work Double Seed St Patt over next 5 sts, then work Stockinette St Patt to end row.

Next Row (RS): Knit across until 2 sts before first marker, K2tog, work Double Seed St Patt over next 5 sts; *with second ball of yarn,* work Double Seed St Patt over next 5 sts, SSK, then knit across to end row.

Repeat last six rows four more times, *and at the same time,* when piece measures same as back to underarms, shape armholes same as for back.

Cont armhole shaping, and work even at neck edge for seven rows as follows: Work Stockinette St Patt until first marker, work Double Seed St Patt over next 5 sts; *with second ball of yarn,* work Double Seed St Patt over next 5 sts, then work Stockinette St Patt to end row.

Next Row (RS): Knit across until 2 sts before first marker, K2tog, work Double Seed St Patt over next 5 sts; *with second ball of yarn,* work Double Seed St Patt over next 5 sts, SSK, then knit across to end row.

Repeat last eight rows once more—20 (20, 21, 21, 22) sts rem each side.

Cont even in patts as established until piece measures approx 24½ (24½, 24½, 25, 25½)" from beg, ending after Row 4 of Double Seed St Patt.

Next Row (RS): K15 (15, 16, 16, 17) sts, slip next 5 sts onto holder; slip next 5 sts onto second holder, *and with second ball of yarn,* knit across to end row.

Dec 1 st each neck edge every row three times—12 (12, 13, 13, 14) sts rem each side.

Work even until piece measures same as back to shoulder, ending after WS row.

Shape Shoulders

Same as for back.

SLEEVES

CO 39 (39, 41, 41, 43) sts. Beg Double Seed St Patt, and work even for eight rows.

Beg Stockinette St Patt, and inc 1 st each side every sixth row 0 (0, 1, 5, 1) times, every eighth row 7 (7, 8, 5, 8) times, then every tenth row 2 (2, 0, 0, 0) times—57 (57, 59, 61, 61) sts.

Cont even until sleeve measures approx 16½ (16½, 17½, 17½, 17½)" from beg, ending after WS row.

Shape Cap

BO 2 (2, 4, 5, 6) sts at beg of next two rows—53 (53, 51, 51, 49) sts rem.

Work fully-fashioned decreases each side every other row 10 (10, 11, 13, 15) times, then every row 9 (9, 7, 5, 2) times—15 sts rem.

BO 2 sts at beg of next four rows.

BO rem 7 sts.

FINISHING

Sew shoulder seams.

Neckband

With RS facing, work Row 1 of Double Seed St Patt across 5 sts from right neck holder, pick up and knit 16 sts along right neck edge, 25 sts along back of neck, 16 sts along left neck edge, and work Row 1 of Double Seed St Patt across 5 sts from left neck holder—67 sts total. Cont even in Double Seed St Patt as established for eight rows.

BO.

With right edge over left edge for cross-over V-neck, whipstitch the five cast-on sts at bottom of neck opening to WS of front.

Set in sleeves.

Sew sleeve and side seams, leaving lower 6" open for side slits.

Michele

Multicolor Knitting 101: Worked in a flattering, vertically aligned slip-stitch pattern, this design uses just one color at a time. You get maximum style with minimum effort!

GAUGE

In Slip St Patt with larger needles, 26 sts and 48 rows = 4". **To save time, take time to check gauge.**

GARTER STITCH

(over any number of sts)

Row 1 (RS): Knit across.

Patt Row: As Row 1.

Repeat Patt Row.

GARTER STITCH STRIPE PATTERN

*Two rows of A, two rows of B. Repeat from * two more times, then work two more rows of A.

SLIP STITCH PATTERN

(mult. 4 + 3 sts)

Row 1 (RS): With B, K1, *slip next st with yarn in back, K3. Repeat from * across, ending row with slip next st with yarn in back, K1.

Row 2: With B, K1, *slip next st with yarn in front, K3. Repeat from * across, ending row with slip next st with yarn in front, K1.

Row 3: With A, *K3, slip next st with yarn in back. Repeat from * across, ending row with K3.

Row 4: With A, *K3, slip next st with yarn in front. Repeat from * across, ending row with K3.

Repeat Rows 1-4 for patt.

NOTE

For sweater assembly, refer to the illustration for set-in construction on page 126.

BACK

With smaller needles and A, CO 103 (111, 117, 132, 140) sts. Beg Garter St Patt, and work even in Garter St Stripe Patt for fourteen rows, inc 8 (8, 10, 11, 11) sts evenly along last row—111 (119, 127, 143, 151) sts.

Change to larger needles and beg Slip St Patt.

Cont even until piece measures approx 10 (10, 10, 10, 10½)" from beg, ending after WS row.

Shape Armholes

BO 4 (4, 6, 8, 8) sts at beg of next two rows—103 (111, 115, 127, 135) sts rem.

Cont patt as established and dec 1 st each side every row 2 (2, 4, 6, 8) times, every other row 2 (4, 4, 8, 8) times, then every fourth row 5 (6, 6, 4, 4) times—85 (87, 87, 91, 95) sts rem.

Cont even until piece measures approx 16½ (17, 17½, 18, 18½)" from beg, ending after WS row.

SKILL LEVEL
Intermediate

SIZES

Extra-Small (Small, Medium, Large, Extra-Large). *Instructions are for smallest size, with changes for other sizes noted in parentheses as necessary.*

FINISHED MEASUREMENTS

Bust: 34 (36½, 39, 44, 46½)"
Total length: 18 (18½, 19, 19½, 20)"

MATERIALS

JCA/Reynolds's *Saucy Sport* (sport weight; 100% cotton; each approx 1¾ oz/50 g and 123 yd/113 m), 5 (6, 6, 7, 7) balls Black #899 (A) and 5 (5, 5, 6, 6) balls Berry #686 (B)

One pair each of sizes 4 and 5 (3.5 and 3.75 mm) knitting needles or size needed to obtain gauge

Stitch holders

Shape Neck

Next Row (RS): Work patt as established across first 19 (20, 20, 22, 24) sts, slip middle 47 sts onto holder; join second ball of yarn and work to end row.

Work both sides at once with separate balls of yarn, and dec 1 st each neck edge every row three times—16 (17, 17, 19, 21) sts rem each side.

Cont even until piece measures approx 17 (17½, 18, 18½, 19)" from beg, ending after WS row.

Shape Shoulders

BO 3 (3, 3, 4, 4) sts each shoulder edge four times, then BO 4 (5, 5, 3, 5) sts each shoulder edge once.

FRONT

Same as back until piece measures approx 13½ (14, 14½, 15, 15½)" from beg, ending after WS row.

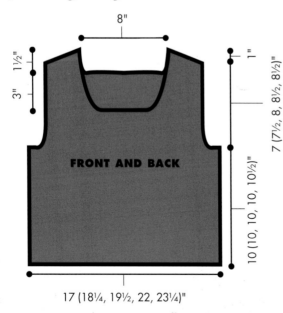

8"

1½"

3"

1"

7 (7½, 8, 8½, 8½)"

FRONT AND BACK

10 (10, 10, 10, 10½)"

17 (18¼, 19½, 22, 23¼)"

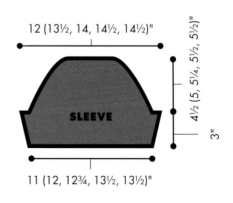

12 (13½, 14, 14½, 14½)"

4½ (5, 5¼, 5½, 5½)"

3"

SLEEVE

11 (12, 12¾, 13½, 13½)"

Shape Neck

Next Row (RS): Work patt as established across first 31 (32, 32, 34, 36) sts, slip middle 23 sts onto holder; join second ball of yarn and work to end row.

Work both sides at once with separate balls of yarn, and BO 3 sts each neck edge once, then BO 2 sts each neck edge once—26 (27, 27, 29, 31) sts rem each side.

Dec 1 st each neck edge every row three times, then every other row seven times—16 (17, 17, 19, 21) sts rem.

Cont even until piece measures same as back to shoulders.

Shape Shoulders

Same as for back.

SLEEVES

With smaller needles and A, CO 66 (73, 77, 81, 81) sts. Beg Garter St Patt, and work even in Garter St Stripe Patt for fourteen rows, inc 5 (6, 6, 6, 6) sts evenly along last row—71 (79, 83, 87, 87) sts.

Change to larger needles, beg Slip St Patt, and inc 1 st each side every other row twice, then every fourth row twice, working new sts into patt as they accumulate—79 (87, 91, 95, 95) sts.

Cont even until piece measures approx 3" from beg, ending after WS row.

Shape Cap

BO 4 (4, 6, 8, 8) sts at beg of next two rows—71 (79, 79, 79, 79) sts rem.

Dec 1 st each side every other row 14 (19, 17, 16, 16) times, then every fourth row 4 (3, 5, 6, 6) times—35 sts rem.

BO 3 sts at beg of next six rows—17 sts rem.

BO.

FINISHING

Sew right shoulder seam.

Neckband

With RS facing, smaller needles, and A, pick up and knit 132 sts around neckline.

Work Garter St Patt until six rows of Garter St Stripe Patt are completed.

Next Row: Cont patt as established, dec 22 sts evenly across—110 sts rem.

Cont patt as established until fourteen rows of Garter St Stripe Patt are completed.

BO *loosely.*

Sew left shoulder seam, including side of neckband.

Set in sleeves. Sew sleeve and side seams.

Gayle

Feminine yet never fussy, here's a modern take on lace! Zigzag borders echo the sweater's wavy lace pattern, while the knit-in vertical band softly frames the neckline.

GAUGE

In Lace Patt with larger needles, 20 sts and 32 rows = 4". **To save time, take time to check gauge.**

BORDER PATTERN

(over mult. 14 + 2 sts)

See chart on page 75.

LACE PATTERN

(over mult. 14 + 2 sts)

See chart on page 75.

V-NECKLINE PATTERN

(over middle 72 sts)

See chart on pages 76–77.

NOTES

SSK = Slip next 2 sts knitwise one at a time, then insert LH needle into the fronts of these 2 sts and knit them tog from this position.

SSSK = Slip next 3 sts knitwise one at a time, then insert LH needle into the fronts of these 3 sts and knit them tog from this position.

For sweater assembly, refer to the illustration for square indented construction on page 126.

BACK

With smaller needles, CO 100 (128) sts. Beg Border Patt, and work even until piece measures approx 1½" from beg, ending after WS row.

Change to larger needles and beg Lace Patt.

Cont even until piece measures approx 17 (16½") from beg, ending after WS row.

Shape Armholes

BO 14 sts at beg of next two rows—72 (100) sts rem.

Cont even until piece measures approx 25" from beg, ending after WS row.

Shape Neck

Next Row (RS): Work in patt as established across first 17 (31) sts; join second skein of yarn and BO middle 38 sts, work to end row.

Work both sides at once with separate skeins of yarn until piece measures approx 25½" from beg, ending after WS row.

SKILL LEVEL

Advanced

SIZES

Small/Medium (Large/Extra-Large). *Instructions are for smallest size, with changes for other size noted in parentheses as necessary.*

FINISHED MEASUREMENTS

Bust: 40 (51)"
Total length: 26½"

MATERIALS

Brown Sheep Company's *Cotton Fleece* (sport weight; 80% pima cotton/ 20% merino wool; each approx 3½ oz/100 g and 215 yd/197 m), 7 (8) skeins Blush #CW660

One pair each of sizes 5 and 6 (3.75 and 4 mm) knitting needles or size needed to obtain gauge

Shape Shoulders

BO 4 (8) sts each shoulder edge three times, then BO 5 (7) sts each shoulder edge once.

FRONT

Same as back until piece measures approx 19½" from beg, ending after Row 8 of Lace Patt.

Shape Neck

Next Row (RS): Work Row 1 of V-Neckline Patt as follows: Work patt as established across first 31 (45) sts, K2tog, P1, K1, P1; join second skein of yarn, P1, K1, P1, SSK, work patt as established to end row.

Work both sides at once with separate skeins of yarn until Row 44 of V-Neckline Patt is completed.

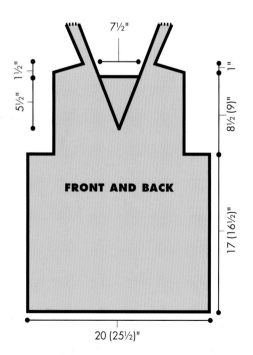

FRONT AND BACK

7½"

1½"

5½"

1"

8½ (9)"

17 (16½)"

20 (25½)"

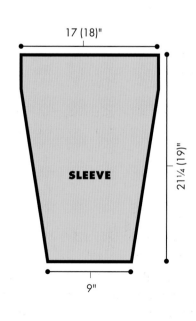

SLEEVE

17 (18)"

21¼ (19)"

9"

BORDER PATTERN

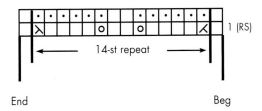

14-st repeat

End   Beg

LACE PATTERN

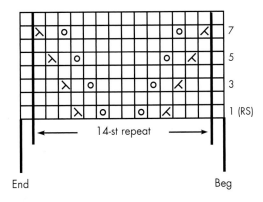

7
5
3
1 (RS)

14-st repeat

End   Beg

KEY

☐ = K on RS; P on WS

• = P on RS; K on WS

o = Yarn over

⟨ = K2tog

⟩ = SSK

Work even in patts as established until piece measures same as back to shoulders.

Shape Shoulders

Work both sides at once with separate skeins of yarn and shape shoulders same as for back—3 sts rem each side.

Work even in patt as established until ribbed pieces, when slightly stretched, meet at center back of neck.

BO.

SLEEVES

With smaller needles, CO 44 sts. Beg Border Patt, and cont even in patt until piece measures approx 1½" from beg, ending after WS row.

Change to larger needles, beg Lace Patt, and inc 1 st each side every fourth row 0 (9) times, then every sixth row 15 (14) times, then every eighth row 6 (0) times—86 (90) sts.

HOT TIP

To make sleeve increases easy while still maintaining the Lace Pattern, place markers on your knitting needles to indicate the last *complete* pattern repeat. Work plain stockinette stitch (or some other unobtrusive pattern) outside the markers until you increase enough new stitches to add another full repeat of the Lace Pattern.

Cont even until piece measures approx 21¼ (19)" from beg, ending after WS row.

BO.

FINISHING

Sew shoulder seams.

Sew sides of neckband ribs to neckline. Sew bind-off edges of neckbands tog at back of neck.

Set in sleeves. Sew sleeve and side seams.

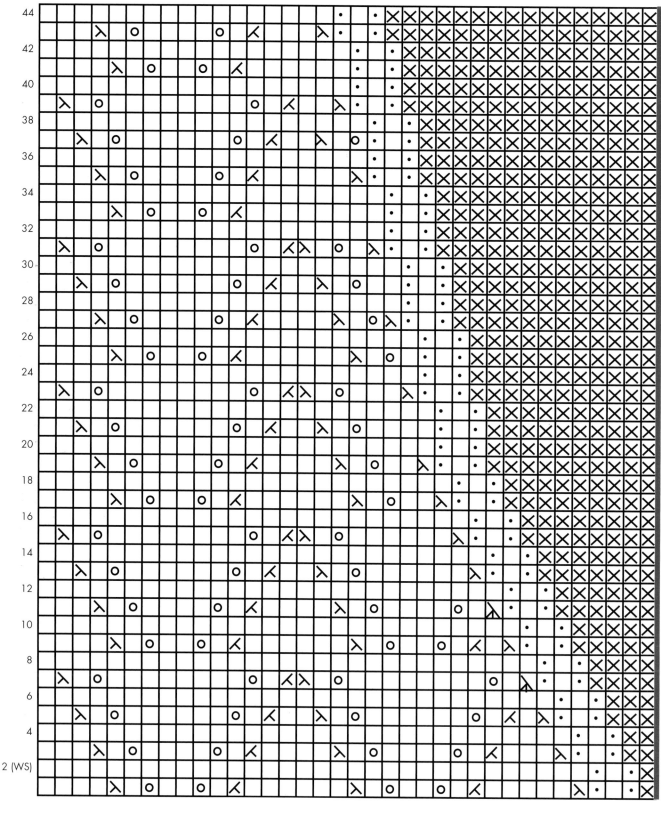

KEY

☐ = K on RS; P on WS

• = P on RS; K on WS

o = Yarn over

⟋ = K2tog

⟍ = SSK

⟑ = K3tog

⟋⟍ = SSSK

✕ = No stitch

NOTE: Red lines mark center of neckline; use separate skeins of yarn for each side of neckline.

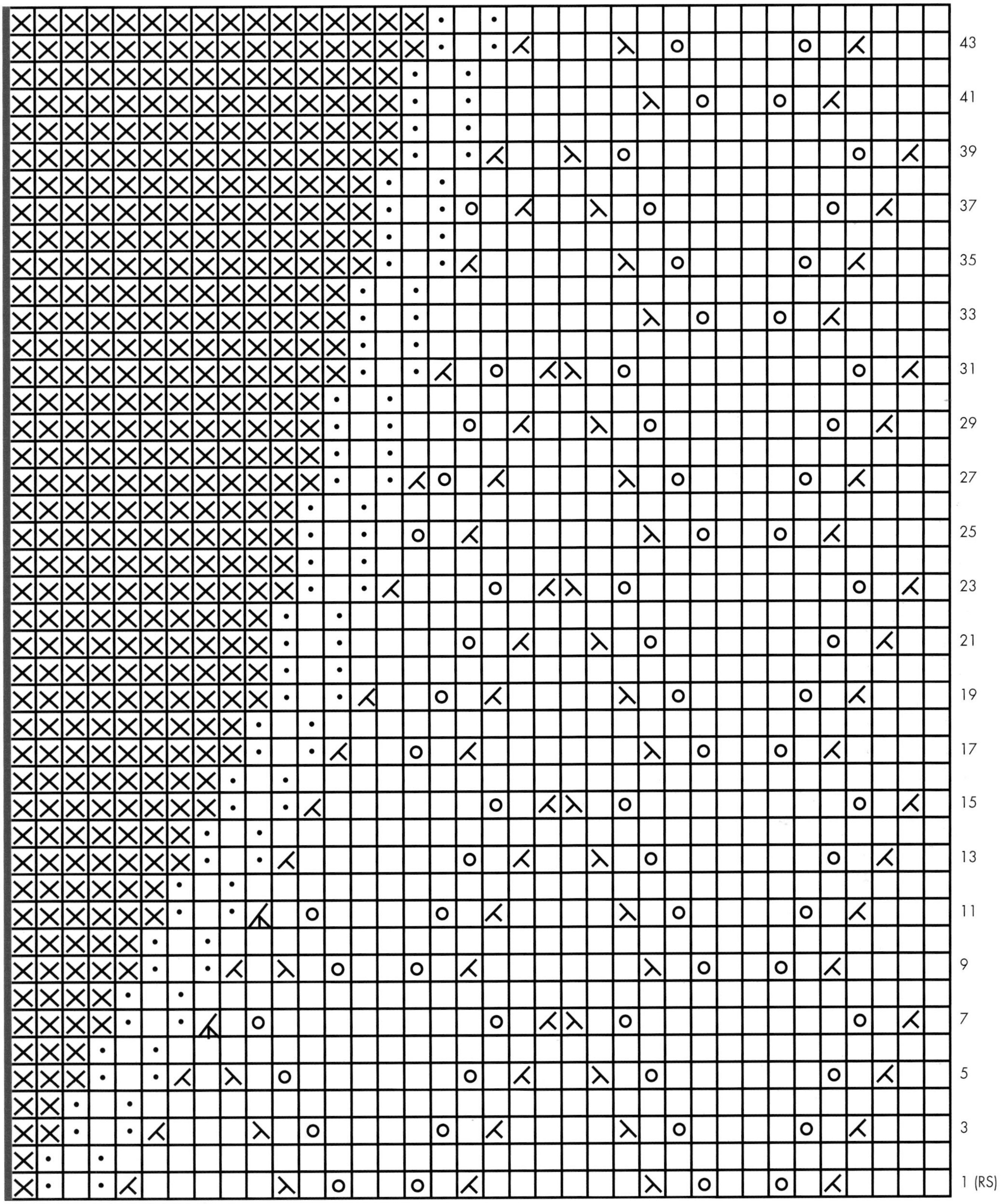

Sarah

Here's a best bet for summer knitting (and wearing!): a casual, cropped pullover with a refreshing mix of stripes. Style and comfort all in one!

GAUGE

In Stockinette St Patt with larger needles, 24 sts and 30 rows = 4". *To save time, take time to check gauge.*

K1 P1 RIB PATTERN
(over mult. 2 sts)

Row 1 (RS): *K1, P1. Repeat from * across.

Patt Row: As Row 1.

Repeat Patt Row for patt.

STOCKINETTE STITCH PATTERN
(over any number of sts)

Row 1 (RS): Knit across.

Row 2: Purl across.

Repeat Rows 1 and 2 for patt.

STRIPE PATTERN FOR FRONT AND BACK

Ten rows *each* of *B, A, C, A. Repeat from * for patt.

STRIPE PATTERN FOR SLEEVES

Six rows *each* of *B, A. Repeat from * for patt.

NOTES

For fully-fashioned decreases:
on RS rows: K1, SSK, work across in patt as established until 3 sts rem in row, ending row with K2tog, K1;
on WS rows: P1, P2tog, work across in patt as established until 3 sts rem in row, ending row with P2tog *through their back loops*, P1.

For fully-fashioned increases: Work 1 st, M1, work across until 1 st rem in row, ending row with M1, work last st.

SSK = Slip next 2 sts knitwise one at a time, then insert LH needle into the fronts of these 2 sts and knit them tog from this position.

M1 = Insert LH needle under the horizontal thread that is between st just worked and the next st, and knit into the back of it.

For sweater assembly, refer to the illustration for set-in construction on page 126.

SKILL LEVEL
Advanced Beginner

SIZES
Small (Medium, Large, Extra-Large). *Instructions are for smallest size, with changes for other sizes noted in parentheses as necessary.*

FINISHED MEASUREMENTS
Bust: 36 (40, 44, 48)"
Total length: 18 (18½, 19, 20)"

MATERIALS
Classic Elite's *Premiere* (sport weight; 50% pima cotton/50% Tencel®; each approx 1¾ oz/50 g and 108 yd/99 m), 5 (5, 6, 7) hanks Lavender #5256 (A), and 3 (3, 4, 4) hanks *each* of Seafoam #5226 (B) and Key Lime #5235 (C)

One pair each of sizes 4 and 5 (3.5 and 3.75 mm) knitting needles or size needed to obtain gauge

BACK

With smaller needles and A, CO 90 (102, 112, 118) sts. Work K1 P1 Rib Patt until piece measures approx 1½" from beg, ending after WS row.

Change to larger needles, beg Stockinette St Patt and Stripe Patt with B, and work even until piece measures approx 3" from beg, ending after WS row.

Increase for Bust

Cont in Stripe Patt, work fully-fashioned increases each side every fourth row 3 (3, 6, 13) times, then every sixth row 6 (6, 4, 0) times—108 (120, 132, 144) sts.

Cont even until piece measures approx 10 (10, 10, 11)" from beg, ending after WS row.

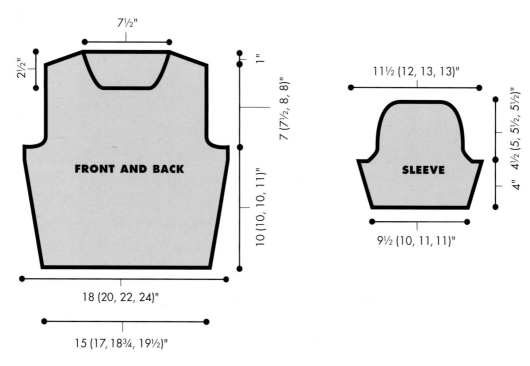

FRONT AND BACK

7½"

2½"

1"

7 (7½, 8, 8)"

10 (10, 10, 11)"

18 (20, 22, 24)"

15 (17, 18¾, 19½)"

SLEEVE

11½ (12, 13, 13)"

4 (4½, 5, 5½)"

9½ (10, 11, 11)"

Shape Armholes

BO 4 (4, 6, 6) sts at beg of next two rows, BO 3 (3, 4, 5) sts at beg of next two rows, then BO 2 (2, 3, 3) sts at beg of next two rows—90 (102, 106, 116) sts rem.

Work fully-fashioned decreases each side every row 2 (9, 10, 16) times, then every other row 4 (2, 2, 0) times—78 (80, 82, 84) sts rem.

Cont even until piece measures approx 17 (17½, 18, 19)" from beg, ending after WS row.

Shape Shoulders

BO 4 (4, 5, 5) sts each shoulder edge three times, then BO 5 (6, 4, 5) sts each shoulder edge once.

BO rem 44 sts for back of neck.

FRONT

Same as back until piece measures approx 15½ (16, 16½, 17½)" from beg, ending after WS row.

Shape Neck

Next Row (RS): K27 (28, 29, 30) sts; join second ball of yarn and BO middle 24 sts, cont patt as established to end row.

Work both sides at once with separate balls of yarn, and BO 3 sts each neck edge once, then BO 2 sts each neck edge once—22 (23, 24, 25) sts rem each side.

Work fully-fashioned decreases each neck edge every row four times, then every other row once—17 (18, 19, 20) sts rem each side.

Cont even, if necessary, until piece measures same as back to shoulders, ending after WS row.

Shape Shoulders
Same as back.

SLEEVES

With smaller needles and A, CO 56 (60, 66, 66) sts. Work K1 P1 Rib Patt until piece measures approx ¾" from beg, ending after WS row.

Change to larger needles, beg Stockinette St Patt and Stripe Patt with B, and work fully-fashioned increases each side every other row 6 (4, 4, 4) times, then every fourth row 1 (2, 2, 2) times—70 (72, 78, 78) sts.

Cont even until piece measures approx 4" from beg, ending after WS row.

Shape Cap

BO 4 (4, 6, 6) sts at beg of next two rows—62 (64, 66, 66) sts rem.

Work fully-fashioned decreases each side every

fourth row 1 (2, 3, 3) times, then every other row 12 times—36 sts rem.

BO 3 sts at beg of next four rows—24 sts rem.

BO.

FINISHING
Sew left shoulder seam.

Neckband

With RS facing, smaller needles, and A, pick up and knit 110 sts around neckline.

Work K1 P1 Rib Patt until band measures approx 1" from beg. BO *loosely* in rib.

Sew right shoulder seam, including side of neckband.

Set in sleeves. Sew sleeve and side seams.

Barbara

Don't you deserve some luxury? Treat yourself to this sweater! Its fine couture details—neatly set-in sleeves, interior waist shaping, and graceful portrait neckline—combined with kitten-soft angora, make you look as good as you feel!

GAUGE

In Stockinette St Patt with smallest needles, 22 sts and 30 rows = 4". **To save time, take time to check gauge.**

K1 P1 RIB PATTERN

(over mult. 2+ 1 sts)

Row 1 (RS): P1, *K1, P1. Repeat from * across.

Row 2: K1, *P1, K1. Repeat from * across.

Repeat Rows 1 and 2 for patt.

STOCKINETTE STITCH PATTERN

(over any number of sts)

Row 1 (RS): Knit across.

Row 2: Purl across.

Repeat Rows 1 and 2 for patt.

NOTES

M1 = Insert LH needle under the horizontal thread that is between st just worked and the next st, and knit into the back of it.

SSK = Slip next 2 sts knitwise one at a time, then insert LH needle into the fronts of these 2 sts and knit them tog from this position.

For fully-fashioned decreases:
on RS rows: K2, SSK, work across in patt as established until 4 sts rem in row, ending row with K2tog, K2;
on WS rows: P2, P2tog, work across in patt as established until 4 sts rem in row, ending row with P2tog *through their back loops*, P2.

For sweater assembly, refer to the illustration for set-in construction on page 126.

BACK

With smallest needles, CO 97 (107, 117, 127, 137) sts. Beg K1 P1 Rib Patt, and work even until piece measures approx 1½" from beg, ending after WS row.

Beg Stockinette St Patt, and work even until piece measures approx 3 (3, 3½, 3½, 3½)" from beg, ending after WS row.

Waist Shaping

Next Row (RS): K22 (24, 26, 28, 30) sts, SSK, place marker, K49 (55, 61, 67, 73) sts, place marker, K2tog, K22 (24, 26, 28, 30) sts to end row.

Work five rows even in Stockinette St Patt.

Next Row (RS): Work to first marker, slip marker, SSK, work until 2 sts before second marker, K2tog, slip marker, work to end row.

Repeat last six rows two more times— 89 (99, 109, 119, 129) sts rem.

Work three rows even in Stockinette St Patt.

SKILL LEVEL
Intermediate

SIZES
Extra-Small (Small, Medium, Large, Extra-Large). *Instructions are for smallest size, with changes for other sizes noted in parentheses as necessary.*

FINISHED MEASUREMENTS
Bust: 35 (39, 43, 46, 50)"
Total length: 22 (22½, 22¾, 23, 23½)"

MATERIALS
Tahki/Stacy Charles's *Jolie* (light worsted weight; 70% French angora/30% merino wool; each approx .87 oz/25 g and 108 yd/ 100 m), 11 (12, 12, 13, 14) balls Light Turquoise #015

One pair each of sizes 6, 7, and 8 (4, 4.5, and 5 mm) knitting needles or size needed to obtain gauge

Two stitch holders

Stitch markers

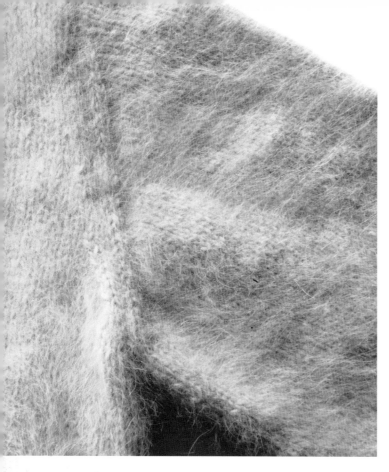

Remove markers, and work even in Stockinette St Patt until piece measures approx 9 (10, 10½, 10½, 11)" from beg, ending after WS row.

Next Row (RS): K24 (26, 28, 30, 32) sts, place marker, M1, K37 (43, 49, 55, 61) sts, M1, place marker, K24 (26, 28, 30, 32) sts to end row—87 (97, 107, 117, 127) sts.

Work three rows even in Stockinette St Patt.

Next Row (RS): Work to first marker, slip marker, M1, work across until next marker, M1, slip marker, work to end row—89 (99, 109, 119, 129) sts.

Repeat last four rows four more times—97 (107, 117, 127, 137) sts.

Remove markers, and cont even in Stockinette St Patt until piece measures approx 13½ (13¾, 13¾, 13½, 13½)" from beg, ending after WS row.

Shape Armholes
BO 2 (3, 4, 5, 6) sts at beg of next two rows—93 (101, 109, 117, 125) sts rem.

Work fully-fashioned decreases each side every row 0 (0, 4, 10, 15) times, every other row 6 (13, 12, 10, 8) times, then every fourth row 3 (0, 0, 0, 0) times—75 (75, 77, 77, 79) sts rem.

Cont even until piece measures approx 19½ (20, 20¼, 20½, 21)" from beg, ending after WS row.

Next Row (RS): Work to first marker, slip marker, SSK, work until 2 sts before second marker, K2tog, slip marker, work to end row.

Repeat last four rows once more—85 (95, 105, 115, 125) sts rem.

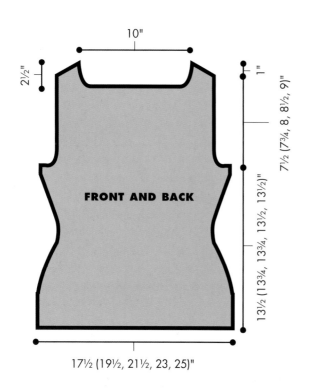

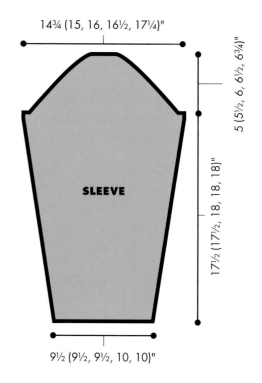

Shape Neck

Next Row (RS): K27 (27, 28, 28, 29) sts; slip middle 21 sts onto holder, join second ball of yarn and work to end row.

Work both sides at once with separate balls of yarn, and BO 5 sts each neck edge once, BO 4 sts each neck edge twice, then BO 2 sts each neck edge once—12 (12, 13, 13, 14) sts rem each side.

Dec 1 st each neck edge every row twice—10 (10, 11, 11, 12) sts rem each side.

Cont even until piece measures approx 21 (21½, 21¾, 22, 22½)" from beg, ending after WS row.

Shape Shoulders

BO 3 (3, 4, 4, 4) sts each shoulder edge twice, then BO rem 4 (4, 3, 3, 4) sts each shoulder edge.

FRONT

Same as back.

SLEEVES

With smallest needles, CO 53 (53, 53, 55, 55) sts. Beg K1 P1 Rib Patt, and work even until piece measures approx 1½" from beg, ending after RS row.

Beg Stockinette St Patt, and inc 1 st each side every fourth row 0 (0, 0, 0, 2) times, every sixth row 0 (4, 10, 14, 18) times, then every eighth row 14 (11, 7, 4, 0) times—81 (83, 87, 91, 95) sts.

Cont even until sleeve measures approx 17½ (17½, 18, 18, 18)" from beg, ending after WS row.

Shape Cap

BO 2 (3, 4, 5, 6) sts at beg of next two rows—77 (77, 79, 81, 83) sts rem.

Work fully-fashioned decreases each side every other row 3 (7, 9, 12, 13) times, then every row 25 (21, 20, 18, 18) times—21 sts rem.

BO 2 sts at beg of next four rows.

BO rem 13 sts.

FINISHING

Sew right shoulder seam.

Collar

With RS facing and smallest needles, pick up and knit 130 sts around neckline, including sts from holders. Work even in Stockinette St Patt until collar measures approx 2" from beg, ending after WS row.

Change to size 7 needles, and work even in Stockinette St Patt until collar measures approx 5" from beg, ending after WS row.

Change to size 8 needles, and work even in Stockinette St Patt until collar measures approx 6½" from beg, ending after WS row.

Next Row (RS): *K1, P1. Repeat from * across.

Next Row: *P1, K1. Repeat from * across.

Repeat last two rows until collar measures approx 7½" from beg.

BO *loosely* in rib.

Sew left shoulder seam, including side of collar.

Set in sleeves. Sew sleeve and side seams.

Maria

Roomy and relaxed, this tunic features slits at both the lower side seams and cuffs. A simple two-row stitch pattern provides texture, and beautiful hand-painted yarn adds a wonderful glow. Its style is nearly effortless!

GAUGE

In Textured Patt with straight needles, 28 sts and 42 rows = 4". **To save time, take time to check gauge.**

TEXTURED PATTERN

(over mult. 2 + 1 sts)

Row 1 (WS): *P1, K1. Repeat from * across, ending row with P1.

Row 2: *K1, P1. Repeat from * across, ending row with K1.

Row 3: Knit across.

Row 4: Knit across.

Repeat Rows 1-4 for patt.

GARTER STITCH PATTERN

(over any number of sts)

Patt Row: Knit.

Repeat Patt Row.

NOTES

SSK = Slip next 2 sts knitwise one at a time, then insert LH needle into the fronts of these 2 sts and knit them tog from this position.

Constructionwise, sleeve cuff is made in two pieces.

For sweater assembly, refer to the illustration for set-in construction on page 126.

BACK

With straight needles, CO 133 (147, 161, 175, 189) sts. Beg Textured Patt, and work even until piece measures approx 17½ (17½, 18, 18, 18)" from beg, ending after WS row.

Shape Armholes

BO 4 (6, 8, 10, 12) sts at beg of next two rows—125 (135, 145, 155, 165) sts rem.

BO 2 sts at beg of next two (two, four, six, six) rows—121 (131, 137, 143, 153) sts rem.

Dec 1 st each side every row 0 (6, 10, 10, 16) times, then every other row 10 (11, 8, 11, 8) times, then every fourth row 2 (0, 0, 0, 0) times—97 (97, 101, 101, 105) sts rem.

Cont even in patt as established until piece measures approx 24½ (24½, 25, 25½, 26)" from beg, ending after WS row.

SKILL LEVEL

Intermediate

SIZES

Small (Medium, Large, Extra-Large, Extra-Extra Large). *Instructions are for smallest size, with changes for other sizes noted in parentheses as necessary.*

FINISHED MEASUREMENTS

Bust: 38 (42, 46, 50, 54)"
Total length: 26 (26, 26½, 27, 27½)"

MATERIALS

Cherry Tree Hill Yarns's *Silk Merino DK* (sport weight; 50% silk/50% wool; each approx 4 oz/113 g and 313 yd/286 m), 8 (8, 9, 9, 10) hanks Wild Cherry

One pair of size 5 (3.75 mm) knitting needles or size needed to obtain gauge

16" Circular knitting needle, size 4 (3.5 mm)

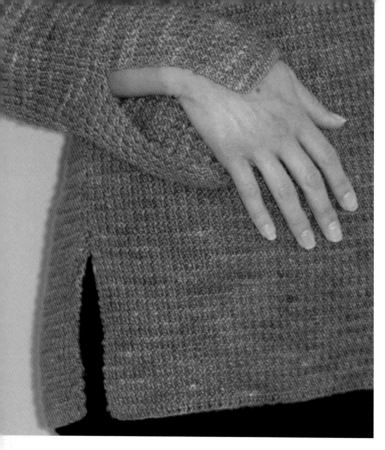

Cont even, if necessary, until piece measures approx 25 (25, 25½, 26, 26½)" from beg, ending after WS row.

Shape Shoulders
BO 5 (5, 5, 5, 6) sts each shoulder edge four times, then BO 4 (4, 6, 6, 4) sts each shoulder edge once.

FRONT
Same as back until piece measures approx 23 (23, 23½, 24, 24½)" from beg, ending after WS row.

Shape Neck
Next Row (RS): Work patt as established across first 38 (38, 40, 40, 42) sts; join second ball of yarn and BO middle 21 sts, work patt as established to end row.

Work both sides at once with separate balls of yarn, and BO 2 sts each neck edge twice—34 (34, 36, 36, 38) sts rem each side.

Dec 1 st each neck edge every row four times, then every other row six times—24 (24, 26, 26, 28) sts rem.

Cont even until piece measures same as back to shoulders.

Shape Shoulders
Same as for back.

SLEEVES
Right Half of Cuff
With straight needles, CO 35 sts. Beg Textured Patt, and work even for 10 rows.

SHAPE NECK
Next Row (RS): Work patt as established across first 26 (26, 28, 28, 30) sts; join second ball of yarn and BO middle 45 sts, work patt as established to end row.

Work both sides at once with separate balls of yarn, and dec 1 st each neck edge every row twice—24 (24, 26, 26, 28) sts rem each side.

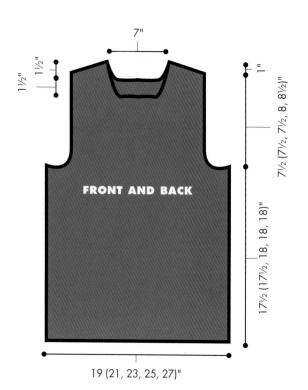

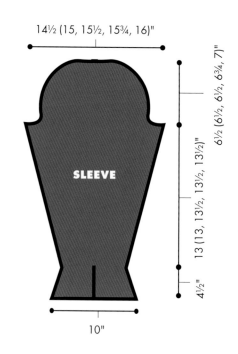

Next Row (WS): Cont in Textured Patt, and dec 1 st at beg of row.

Next Nine Rows: Work even in patt as established.

Repeat last ten rows three more times—31 sts rem.

Cont even until piece measures approx 4½" from beg, ending after WS row.

Slip sts onto holder.

Left Half of Cuff
Same as right half of cuff, *except* reverse shaping.

Joining after Cuff
With RS facing, cont patt as established and work across right half of cuff, inc 1 st in last st—32 sts; cont patt across left half of cuff—63 sts total.

Cont patt as established, inc 1 st each side every fourth row 0 (2, 4, 7, 10) times, every sixth row 15 (19, 19, 17, 15) times, then every eighth row 4 (0, 0, 0, 0) times—101 (105, 109, 111, 113) sts.

Cont even until piece measures approx 17½ (17½, 18, 18, 18)" from beg, ending after WS row.

Shape Cap
BO 4 (6, 8, 10, 12) sts at beg of next two rows—93 (93, 93, 91, 89) sts rem.

Dec 1 st each side every other row 26 (26, 26, 30, 32) times, then every row 8 (8, 8, 3, 0) times—25 sts rem.

BO 2 sts at beg of next six rows—13 sts rem.

BO.

FINISHING
Sew left shoulder seam.

Neckband
With RS facing and circular needle, pick up and knit 84 sts around neckline. Beg Garter St Patt, and work even until band measures approx 1" from beg.

BO.

Sew right shoulder seam, including side of neckband.

Set in sleeves.

Sew sleeve seams and side seams, leaving lower 4½" open for side slits.

HOT TIP

To ensure random color throughout when using multi-colored yarn, work from two balls of yarn simultaneously, alternating balls every two rows and carrying the yarn not in use *loosely* along the side of the fabric on the WS. No unsightly color blotches!

Cynthia

Sleek and chic, this cabled shell features clean, self-finished armbands on a body-conscious, tapered silhouette. Perfectly elegant!

GAUGE

In Stockinette St Patt with larger needles, 18 sts and 25 rows = 4". *To save time, take time to check gauge.*

K1 P1 RIB PATTERN

(over mult. 2 sts)

Patt Row: *K1, P1. Repeat from * across.

Repeat Patt Row.

STOCKINETTE STITCH PATTERN

(over any number of sts)

Row 1 (RS): Knit across.

Row 2: Purl across.

Repeat Rows 1 and 2 for patt.

CABLE PANEL

(over middle 10 sts)

See chart on page 93.

NOTES

SSK = Slip next 2 sts knitwise one at a time, then insert LH needle into the fronts of these 2 sts and knit them tog from this position.

For fully-fashioned decreases:
on RS rows: (K1, P1) three times, SSK, work even in patts as established until 8 sts rem, ending row with K2tog, (P1, K1) three times; *on WS rows:* (P1, K1) three times, P2tog, work even in patts as established until 8 sts rem, ending row with P2tog *through their back loops*, (K1, P1) three times.

BACK

With smaller needles, CO 72 (76, 80, 84) sts. Beg K1 P1 Rib Patt, and work even until piece measures approx 1½" from beg.

Next Row (RS): Change to larger needles, work Row 1 of Stockinette St Patt over first 31 (33, 35, 37) sts, place marker, work Row 1 of Cable Panel over middle 10 sts, place marker, work Row 1 of Stockinette St Patt to end row.

Cont patts as established, and inc 1 st each side every fourteenth (fourteenth, tenth, tenth) row 4 (4, 5, 5) times—80 (84, 90, 94) sts.

Work even in patts as established until piece measures approx 13¾ (13¼, 13, 12¾)" from beg, ending after WS row.

Shape Armholes

Next Row (RS): Work fully-fashioned decreases each side.

Cont patts as established, and work fully-fashioned decreases each side every row 0 (1, 3, 3) more times, then every other row 9 (9, 9, 10) times—60 (62, 64, 66) sts.

SKILL LEVEL
Intermediate

SIZES
Small (Medium, Large, Extra-Large). *Instructions are for smallest size, with changes for other sizes noted in parentheses as necessary.*

FINISHED MEASUREMENTS
Bust: 34 (36, 38, 40)"
Total length: 22"

MATERIALS
JCA/Reynolds's *Cabaret* (heavy worsted weight; 100% cotton; each approx 1¾ oz/50 g and 78 yd/71 m), 8 (9, 10, 11) balls Butter #6152

One pair each of sizes 7 and 8 (4.5 and 5.0 mm) knitting needles or size needed to obtain gauge

16" Circular knitting needles, sizes 6 and 7 (4.0 and 4.5 mm)

Cable needle

Stitch markers

Cont even in patts as established until piece measures approx 20¾" from beg, ending after Row 8 of Cable Panel.

Shape Shoulders

BO 3 (3, 4, 4) sts each shoulder edge three times, then BO 4 (5, 3, 4) sts each shoulder edge once.

Slip rem 34 sts onto holder.

FRONT

Same as back until piece measures approx 19½" from beg, ending after Row 16 of Cable Panel.

Shape Neck

Next Row (RS): Work across first 20 (21, 22, 23) sts, slip middle 20 sts onto holder for front of neck; join second ball of yarn and work to end row.

Work both sides at once with separate balls of yarn and BO 3 sts each neck edge once, then BO 2 sts each neck edge once—15 (16, 17, 18) sts rem each side.

Dec 1 st at each neck edge every row twice—13 (14, 15, 16) sts rem each side.

Cont even until piece measures same as back to shoulders.

Shape Shoulders

Same as for back.

FINISHING

Sew shoulder seams.

Neckband

With RS facing and larger circular needle, beg at right shoulder seam, and working on sts from back neck holder, K12, work Row 1 of Cable Panel across next 10 sts, K12; pick up and knit 14 sts along left side of neckline; working on sts from front neck holder, K5, work Row 1 of Cable Panel across next 10 sts, K5; pick up and knit 14 sts along right side of neckline—82 sts total.

Cont even in patts as established until neckband measures approx 2½" from beg, ending after Row 15 of Cable Panel.

Neckband Facing

Change to smaller circular needle, discontinue Cable Panel, and cont even, knitting all sts, until band measures approx 5" from beg.

BO *loosely*.

Fold neckband facing to WS and *loosely* whipstitch into place.

Sew side seams.

CABLE PANEL

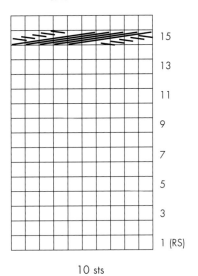

15
13
11
9
7
5
3
1 (RS)

10 sts

KEY

☐ = K on RS; P on WS

= Slip next 5 sts onto cn and hold in back; K5; K5 from cn

Kirstin

Here's an update to your favorite weekend classic: a cozy woolly hoodie! Include the two-way zipper for extra style.

GAUGE

In Stockinette St Patt, 15 sts and 20 rows = 4". **To save time, take time to check gauge.**

SEED STITCH PATTERN

(over mult. 2 + 1 sts)

Row 1 (RS): P1, *K1, P1. Repeat from * across.

Row 2: As Row 1.

Repeat Rows 1 and 2 for patt.

STOCKINETTE STITCH PATTERN

(over any number of sts)

Row 1 (RS): Knit across.

Row 2: Purl across.

Repeat Rows 1 and 2 for patt.

NOTES

Throughout, instructions include one selvage st each side; these sts are not reflected in final measurements.

SSK = Slip next 2 sts knitwise one at a time, then insert LH needle into the fronts of these 2 sts and knit them tog from this position.

For fully-fashioned decreases:
on RS rows: K3, SSK, work across in patt as established until 5 sts rem in row, ending row with K2tog, K3;
on WS rows: P3, P2tog, work across in patt as established until 5 sts rem in row, ending row with P2tog *through their back loops*, P3.

M1 = Insert LH needle under the horizontal thread that is between st just worked and the next st, and knit into the back of it.

For sweater assembly, refer to the illustration for raglan construction on page 126.

BACK

CO 65 (71, 77, 83, 89) sts. Beg Seed St Patt, and work even until piece measures approx 1½" from beg, ending after WS row.

Next Row (RS): Beg Stockinette St Patt, and inc 1 st at beg of row—66 (72, 78, 84, 90) sts.

Work even until piece measures approx 12½ (11½, 13, 12½, 12½)" from beg, ending after WS row.

Shape Raglan

Work fully-fashioned decreases each side every other row 18 (19, 18, 19, 16) times, then every row 2 (4, 8, 10, 16) times—26 sts rem.

BO.

LEFT FRONT

CO 33 (35, 39, 41, 45) sts.

Beg Seed St Patt, and work even until piece measures approx 1½" from beg, ending after WS row.

Next Row (RS): Inc 0 (1, 0, 1, 0) st at beg of row, and work Row 1 of Stockinette St Patt across until 5 sts rem in row, place marker, work Row 1 of Seed St Patt over last 5 sts—33 (36, 39, 42, 45) sts.

SKILL LEVEL
Intermediate

SIZES
Extra-Small (Small, Medium, Large, Extra-Large). *Instructions are for smallest size, with changes for other sizes noted in parentheses as necessary.*

FINISHED MEASUREMENTS
Bust (Zipped): 33½ (36¾, 40¼, 43½, 46½)"
Total length: 20 (20, 22, 22, 22)"

MATERIALS
Classic Elite's *Beatrice* (bulky weight; 100% merino wool; each approx 1¾ oz/ 50 g and 63 yd/58 m), 17 (19, 20, 22, 23) balls Orange #3285

One pair of size 10 (6 mm) knitting needles or size needed to obtain gauge

Two size 10 (6 mm) double-pointed knitting needles

18 (18, 20, 20, 20)" Separating zipper

Two stitch holders

Stitch marker

Next Row (WS): Work Row 2 of Seed St Patt across first 5 sts, work Row 2 of Stockinette St Patt across to end row.

Repeat last two rows until piece measures approx 12½ (11½, 13, 12½, 12½)" from beg, ending after WS row.

Shape Raglan

Cont patt as established, working fully-fashioned decreases at armhole edge same as for back until piece measures approx 18 (18, 20, 20, 20)" from beg, ending after WS row.

Shape Neck

Cont armhole decreases same as for back, *and at the same time,* slip 5 sts at neck edge onto holder.

BO 3 sts at neck edge once, then BO 2 sts at neck edge twice, then dec 1 st at neck edge once.

RIGHT FRONT

Same as left front *except* reverse placement of front band and all shaping.

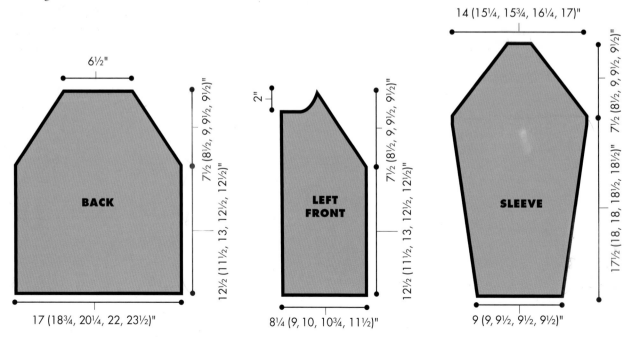

BACK

6½"

7½ (8½, 9, 9½, 9½)"

12½ (11½, 13, 12½, 12½)"

17 (18¾, 20¼, 22, 23½)"

LEFT FRONT

2"

7½ (8½, 9, 9½, 9½)"

12½ (11½, 13, 12½, 12½)"

8¼ (9, 10, 10¾, 11½)"

SLEEVE

14 (15¼, 15¾, 16¼, 17)"

7½ (8½, 9, 9½, 9½)"

17½ (18, 18, 18½, 18½)"

9 (9, 9½, 9½, 9½)"

SLEEVES

CO 35 (35, 37, 37, 37) sts.

Beg Seed St Patt, and work even until piece measures approx 1½" from beg, ending after WS row.

Beg Stockinette St Patt, and inc 1 st each side every fourth row 0 (0, 0, 0, 2) times, then every sixth row 2 (9, 9, 12, 12) times, then every eighth row 8 (3, 3, 1, 0) times—55 (59, 61, 63, 65) sts.

Work even until piece measures approx 17½ (18, 18, 18½, 18½)" from beg, ending after WS row.

Shape Raglan

Work fully-fashioned decreases each side every other row 15 (17, 18, 21, 20) times, then every row 8 (8, 8, 6, 8) times—9 sts rem.

BO.

FINISHING

Sew raglan seams.

HOOD

With RS facing, pick up and knit 5 sts from right front neck holder, 9 sts along right front neck, 9 sts along top of sleeve, 26 sts along back of neck, 9 sts along top of sleeve, 9 sts along left front neck, and 5 sts from left front neck holder—72 sts total.

Cont to work first and last 5 sts in Seed St Patt, work rem sts in Stockinette St Patt, and work even for five rows.

Next Row (RS): Cont patts as established across first 35 sts, M1, K2, M1, work patts as established to end row—74 sts.

Work even in patts as established for seven rows.

Next Row (RS): Cont patts as established across first 36 sts, M1, K2, M1, work patts as established to end row—76 sts.

Work even in patts as established for seven rows.

Next Row (RS): Cont patts as established across first 37 sts, M1, K2, M1, work patts as established to end row—78 sts.

Work even in patts as established until hood measures approx 12" from beg, ending after WS row.

Next Row (RS): Cont patts as established across first 36 sts, SSK, K2, K2tog, work patts as established to end row—76 sts.

Work even in patts as established for one row.

Next Row (RS): Cont patts as established across first 35 sts, SSK, K2, K2tog, work patts as established to end row—74 sts.

Work even in patts as established for one row.

Next Row (RS): Cont patts as established across first 34 sts, SSK, K2, K2tog, work patts as established to end row—72 sts.

Work even in patts as established for one row.

Next Row (RS): Cont patts as established across first 33 sts, SSK, K2, K2tog, work patts as established to end row—70 sts.

Divide rem sts onto two double-pointed needles, putting 35 sts onto each one, and holding WS facing each other, graft them tog.

Sew underarm and side seams.

Sew in zipper.

Emily

Here's your new summer favorite: a great-fitting bandeau shaped to fit with subtle bust darts and concealed elastic. Perfect for summer heat!

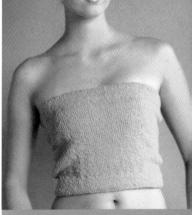

GAUGE

In Stockinette St Patt, *unstretched*, with larger needle, 24 sts and 34 rnds = 4".
To save time, take time to check gauge.

STOCKINETTE STITCH PATTERN

(over any number of sts)
Patt Rnd (RS): Knit around.

Repeat Patt Rnd.

NOTES

For best fit, these finished measurements have *negative* ease, causing fabric to stretch and conform to the body.

Constructionwise, this design is made circularly in one piece.

M1 = Insert LH needle under the horizontal thread that is between st just worked and the next st, and knit into the back of it.

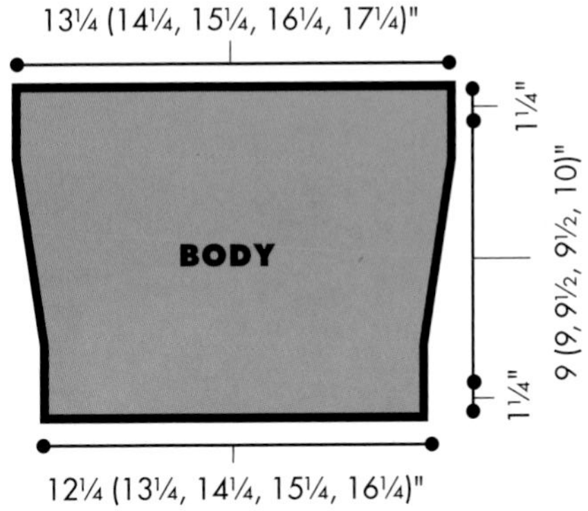

BODY

With smaller needle, CO 146 (158, 170, 182, 194) sts. Join, being careful not to twist sts. Place marker onto needle for beg of rnd.

Beg Stockinette St Patt, and work even until piece measures approx 1¼" from beg.

Foldline Rnd: Purl around.

Change to larger needle, and cont Stockinette St Patt until piece measures approx 2½" from Foldline Rnd.

Next Rnd: K18 (21, 24, 27, 30) sts, place marker, K36 sts, place marker, knit to end rnd.

Dart Inc Rnd: Knit to first marker, M1, slip marker, K36, slip marker, M1, knit to end of rnd—148 (160, 172, 184, 196) sts.

Cont in Stockinette St Patt, and repeat Dart Inc Rnd every sixth rnd five more times—158 (170, 182, 194, 206) sts.

Cont even until piece measures approx 9 (9, 9½, 9½, 10)" from Foldline Rnd.

Repeat Foldline Rnd.

Change to smaller needle, and cont even in Stockinette St Patt until piece measures approx 1¼" from second Foldline Rnd.

BO *loosely.*

FINISHING

Cut two pieces of elastic to desired measurements, adding ½" overlap. Sew ends tog, overlapping ½".

Fold upper and lower facings to WS, encasing elastic, and *loosely* whipstitch into place.

SKILL LEVEL
Advanced Beginner

SIZES
Extra-Small (Small, Medium, Large, Extra-Large).
Instructions are for smallest size, with changes for other sizes noted in parentheses as necessary.

FINISHED MEASUREMENTS
Bust: 26½ (28½, 30½, 32½, 34½)"
Total length: 9 (9, 9½, 9½, 10)"

MATERIALS
Classic Elite Yarn's *Star* (sport weight; 99% cotton/1% Lycra®; each approx 1¾ oz/50 g and 112 yd/103 m), 3 (4, 4, 5, 5) hanks Turquoise #5117

24" Circular knitting needles, sizes 5 and 7 (3.75 and 4.5 mm)

1" wide elastic, approx 2 yd/2 m

Stitch markers

HOT TIP

If you have a tendency to bind off too tightly, use knitting needles that are three sizes larger than the ones used in your project for binding off.

13¼ (14¼, 15¼, 16¼, 17¼)"

BODY

1¼"

9 (9, 9½, 9½, 10)"

1¼"

12¼ (13¼, 14¼, 15¼, 16¼)"

Marnie

You'll find yourself living in this fun and versatile cardigan! With its single button closure and easily made checkerboard fabric, it's wonderfully suited for work and play.

GAUGE

In Textured Patt with larger needles, 20 sts and 28 rows = 4". **To save time, take time to check gauge.**

TEXTURED PATTERN FOR BACK AND SLEEVES

(over mult. 6 + 2 sts)

See chart on page 103.

TEXTURED PATTERN FOR LEFT FRONT

(over mult. 6 + 1 sts)

See chart on page 103.

TEXTURED PATTERN FOR RIGHT FRONT

(over mult. 6 + 1 sts)

See chart on page 103.

NOTE

For sweater assembly, refer to the illustration for square indented construction on page 126.

BACK

With larger needles, CO 86 (98, 110, 122, 134) sts. Beg Textured Patt for Back and Sleeves, and work even until piece measures approx 12½" from beg, ending after WS row.

Shape Armholes

Next Row (RS): Cont patts as established, BO 6 (12, 12, 18, 18) sts at beg of next two rows—74 (74, 86, 86, 98) sts rem.

Cont even until piece measures approx 20½ (21, 21½, 21½, 22)" from beg, ending after WS row.

Shape Shoulders

BO 5 (5, 7, 7, 8) sts at beg of next six rows. BO 5 (5, 5, 5, 8) sts at beg of next two rows—34 sts rem.

BO.

LEFT FRONT

With larger needles, CO 43 (49, 55, 61, 67) sts. Beg Textured Patt for Left Front, and work even until piece measures approx 12½" from beg, ending after WS row.

Shape Armhole

Next Row (RS): BO 6 (12, 12, 18, 18) sts at beg of row, work patt as

SKILL LEVEL

Intermediate

SIZES

Small (Medium, Large, Extra-Large, Extra-Extra Large). *Instructions are for smallest size, with changes for other sizes noted in parentheses as necessary.*

FINISHED MEASUREMENTS

Bust (Buttoned): 34¼ (39½, 44, 49, 54)"

Total length: 21½ (22, 22½, 22½, 23)"

MATERIALS

Muench Yarns's *Samoa* (light worsted weight; 50% cotton/50% microfiber; each approx 1¾ oz/50 g and 104 yd/95 m), 13 (14, 15, 17, 18) balls Kiwi #78

One pair each of sizes 6 and 7 (4 and 4.5 mm) knitting needles or size needed to obtain gauge

Cable needle

One ¾" button (JHB International's *Agoya Fiesta Gold,* Style #70766 was used on sample garment)

established to end row—37 (37, 43, 43, 49) sts rem.

Cont even in patt as established until piece measures approx 19 (19½, 20, 20, 20½)" from beg, ending after RS row.

Next Row (WS): BO 8 sts at beg of row, work in patt as established to end row—29 (29, 35, 35, 41) sts rem.

BO 4 sts at neck edge once, then BO 2 sts at neck edge twice—21 (21, 27, 27, 33) sts rem.

Dec 1 st at neck edge once.

Cont even until piece measures same as back to shoulder, ending after WS row.

Shape Shoulder
BO 5 (5, 7, 7, 8) sts at shoulder edge three times— 5 (5, 5, 5, 8) sts rem.

Work one row even.

BO.

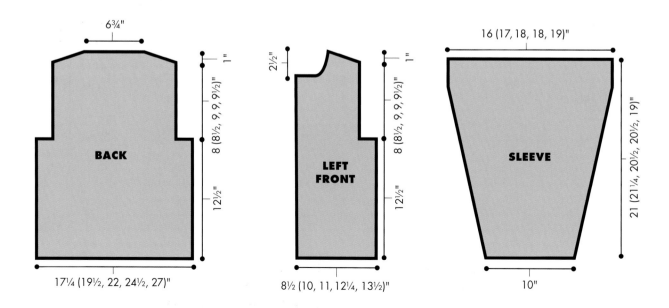

6¾"

1"

8 (8½, 9, 9, 9½)"

12½"

BACK

17¼ (19½, 22, 24½, 27)"

2½"

1"

8 (8½, 9, 9, 9½)"

12½"

LEFT FRONT

8½ (10, 11, 12¼, 13½)"

16 (17, 18, 18, 19)"

21 (21¼, 20½, 20½, 19)"

SLEEVE

10"

RIGHT FRONT

Same as left front *except* work Textured Patt for Right Front and reverse all shaping.

SLEEVES

With larger needles, CO 50 sts. Beg Textured Patt for Back and Sleeves, and inc 1 st each side every fourth row 0 (0, 1, 4, 18) times, every sixth row 0 (10, 19, 16, 5) times, every eighth row 10 (8, 0, 0, 0) times, then every tenth row 5 (0, 0, 0, 0) times—80 (86, 90, 90, 96) sts.

Work even until piece measures approx 21 (21¼, 20½, 20½, 19)" from beg.

BO.

FINISHING

Sew shoulder seams.

Left Front Edging

With RS facing and smaller needles, pick up and knit 94 (96, 98, 98, 100) sts along left front edge.

Next Row (WS): Knit.

Next Row: Purl.

HOT TIP

Prefer a longer, tunic-length cardigan? Easy! Continue knitting even until your back and front pieces measure 18½ (18½, 18½, 19, 19)" before shaping the armholes. Then begin your front neck shaping when the pieces measure 25 (25½, 26, 26½, 27)" from your cast-on edge, and start your shoulder shaping when the pieces measure 26½ (27, 27½, 28, 28½)".

Next Row: Knit to BO.

Right Front Edging

Same as left front edging, except on second row, make one buttonhole ¼" down from beg of neck shaping by binding off 3 sts. On next row, CO 3 sts over the bound-off sts.

Neckband

With RS facing and smaller needles, pick up and knit 90 sts around neckline, including sides of front edging.

Complete same as left front edging.

Set in sleeves. Sew sleeve and side seams.

Sew on button opposite buttonhole.

TEXTURED PATTERN FOR BACK AND SLEEVES

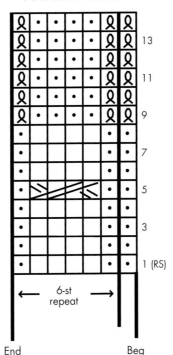

TEXTURED PATTERN FOR LEFT FRONT

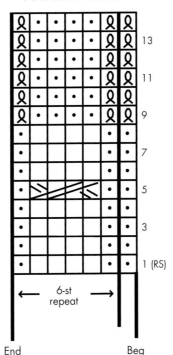

TEXTURED PATTERN FOR RIGHT FRONT

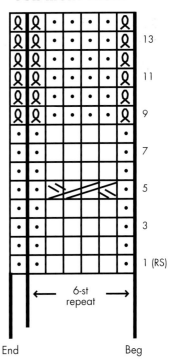

KEY

☐ = K on RS; P on WS

• = P on RS; K on WS

 = Slip next 2 sts onto cn and hold in back; K2; K2 from cn

ℛ = K *through back loop on RS;* P *through back loop on WS*

Lauren

Every stitch counts when knitting at a bulky gauge! Here, ultra-thick roving wool serves as the perfect showcase for an unusual circular cable.

GAUGE

In Reverse Stockinette St Patt, 10 sts and 14 rows = 4". **To save time, take time to check gauge.**

K1 P1 RIB PATTERN

(over mult. 2 sts)

Patt Row: *K1, P1. Repeat from * across.

Repeat Patt Row.

CABLED RIB PATTERN

(over middle 21 sts)

See chart on page 107.

CABLE PANEL

(over middle 27 sts, which increases to 31 sts for Rows 1-15)

See chart on page 107.

REVERSE STOCKINETTE STITCH PATTERN

(over any number of sts)

Row 1 (RS): Purl across.

Row 2: Knit across.

Repeat Rows 1 and 2 for patt.

NOTES

Throughout, instructions include one selvage st each side; these sts are not reflected in final measurements.

M1 = Insert LH needle under the horizontal thread that is between st just worked and the next st, and knit into the back of it.

Central Double Increase (increases from 1 to 3 sts) = Knit into back and then into front of indicated st and slip these 2 new sts off LH needle onto RH needle; insert point of LH needle behind the vertical strand that runs downward between the two sts just made, and knit into the back of it.

For sweater assembly, refer to the illustration for set-in construction on page 126.

BACK

With A, CO 49 (53, 57, 65) sts. Change to B, and set up patt as follows: Work K1 P1 Rib Patt across first 14 (16, 18, 22) sts, place marker, work Row 1 of Cabled Rib Patt over middle 21 sts, place marker, P1, work K1 P1 Rib Patt across next 12 (14, 16, 20) sts, K1. Work even in patts as established until piece measures approx 2" from beg, ending after Row 4 of Cabled Rib Patt.

Next Row (RS): Work Row 1 of Reverse Stockinette St Patt across first 11 (13, 15, 19) sts, place marker, work Row 1 of Cable Panel over middle 27 sts, place marker, work Row 1 of Reverse Stockinette St Patt to end row.

SKILL LEVEL
Advanced

SIZES
Small (Medium, Large, Extra-Large). *Instructions are for smallest size, with changes for other sizes noted in parentheses as necessary.*

FINISHED MEASUREMENTS
Bust: 37 (40, 45, 50)"
Total length: 21"

MATERIALS
Brown Sheep Company's *Burly Spun* (bulky weight; 100% wool; each approx 8 oz/226 g and 132 yd/ 121 m), 1 hank Limeade #BS120 (A) and 6 (6, 6, 7) hanks Periwinkle #BS59 (B)

One pair of size 13 (9 mm) knitting needles or size needed to obtain gauge

Two cable needles

Cont even in patts as established until piece measures approx 5 (4¼, 4, 4)" from beg, ending after WS row.

Cont patts as established, and inc 1 st each side every tenth row 2 (2, 0, 0) times, every eighth row 1 (1, 0, 3) times, then every sixth row 0 (0, 4, 0) times—14 (16, 19, 22) sts to the outside of each marker.

Cont even in patts as established until piece measures approx 13 (12½, 12, 12)" from beg, ending after Row 18 (16, 14, 14) of Cable Panel.

Shape Armholes

Next Row (RS): BO 3 (4, 5, 7) sts at beg of next two rows. Dec 1 st each side every row 2 (2, 3, 4) times, then every other row twice—7 (8, 9, 9) sts rem to the outside of each marker.

Cont even in patts as established until piece measures approx 19" from beg, ending after Row 20 of Cable Panel.

Shape Neck

Next Row (RS): Work patts as established across first 13 (14, 15, 15) sts; join second ball of yarn and BO middle 15 sts, work patts as established to end row.

Work both sides at once with separate balls of yarn, and dec 1 st each neck edge on next row—12 (13, 14, 14) sts rem each side.

BO.

FRONT

Same as back until piece measures approx 18½" from beg, ending after Row 18 of Cable Panel.

Shape Neck

Next Row (RS): Work patts as established across first

15 (16, 17, 17) sts; join second ball of yarn and BO middle 11 sts, work patts as established to end row.

Work both sides at once with separate balls of yarn, and BO 2 sts each neck edge once, then dec 1 st each neck edge once—12 (13, 14, 14) sts rem each side. Cont even until piece measures same as back to shoulders.

BO.

SLEEVES

With A, CO 26 (28, 30, 30) sts. Change to B, and beg K1 P1 Rib Patt. Work even until piece measures approx 2" from beg, ending after WS row.

Next Row (RS): Beg Reverse Stockinette St Patt, and inc 1 st each side every fourth row 0 (0, 1, 1) times, then every sixth row 7 (6, 8, 8) times, then every eighth row 1 (2, 0, 0) times—42 (44, 48, 48) sts.

Cont even until piece measures approx 17½ (18, 18, 18)" from beg, ending after WS row.

Shape Cap

BO 3 (4, 5, 7) sts at beg of next two rows—36 (36, 38, 34) sts rem.

Dec 1 st each side every other row 1 (3, 5, 7) times, then every row 12 (10, 8, 4) times—10 (10, 12, 12) sts rem.

BO 2 sts at beg of next two rows.

BO rem 6 (6, 8, 8) sts.

FINISHING

Sew right shoulder seam.

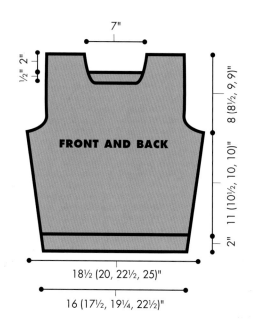

7"
½" 2"
8 (8½, 9, 9)"
11 (10½, 10, 10)"
2"
FRONT AND BACK
18½ (20, 22½, 25)"
16 (17½, 19¼, 22½)"

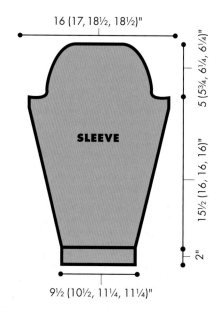

16 (17, 18½, 18½)"
5 (5¾, 6¼, 6¼)"
15½ (16, 16, 16)"
2"
SLEEVE
9½ (10½, 11¼, 11¼)"

Neckband

With RS facing and B, pick up and knit 42 sts around neckline. Work even in K1 P1 Rib Patt until band measures approx 3½" from beg, ending after WS row. Change to A, and work rib to BO.

Sew left shoulder seam, including side of neckband.

Set in sleeves. Sew sleeve and side seams.

HOT TIP

Do you find those X's in the chart confusing? Don't make something out of nothing. Think of them simply as "place markers" that show the location of stitches that have been decreased away in previous rows. Just move your eye beyond the X to the next symbol on the chart and continue knitting.

CABLE PANEL

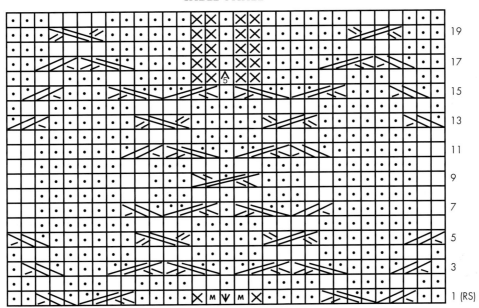

27 sts (increases to 31 sts for Rows 1–15)

CABLED RIB PATTERN

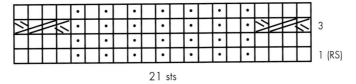

21 sts

KEY

☐ = K on RS; P on WS

• = P on RS; K on WS

= Slip next 2 sts onto cn and hold in back; K2; K2 from cn

= Slip next st onto cn and hold in back; K2; P1 from cn

= Slip next 2 sts onto cn and hold in front; P2; K2 from cn

✕ = No stitch

M = Make one = Lift horizontal running thread between the knitting needles, and place it on LH needle; K into the back of this strand to make 1 st

V = Central Double Increase (increases from 1 to 3 sts) = K into the back and then into the front of indicated st and slip them off LH needle onto RH needle; insert point of LH needle behind the vertical strand that runs downward between the two sts just made, and K into the back of it

= Slip next 2 sts onto cn and hold in back; K2; P2 from cn

= Slip next 2 sts onto cn and hold in front; P1; K2 from cn

= Slip next 2 sts onto cn #1 and hold in back; slip next st onto cn #2 and hold in back; K2; P1 from cn #2; K2 from cn #1

= Slip next 3 sts with yarn in back, drop yarn; *pass the second st on RH needle over the first st on RH needle; slip first st from RH needle back to LH needle; pass the second st on LH needle over the first st on LH needle**; slip first st from LH needle back to RH needle and repeat from * to ** once again; pick up yarn and K remaining st

Pamela
Zip into fashion with this sporty pullover!
Tipped edges on the all-over rib add extra flair.

GAUGE

In Textured Rib Patt, 22 sts and 26 rows = 4". ***To save time, take time to check gauge.***

TEXTURED RIB PATTERN

(over mult. 4 + 1 sts)

Row 1 (RS): K2, *P1, K3. Repeat from * across, ending row with P1, K2.

Row 2: *P1, K3. Repeat from * across, ending row with P1.

Repeat Rows 1 and 2 for patt.

K1 P1 RIB PATTERN

(over mult. 2 + 1 sts)

Row 1 (RS): P1, *K1, P1. Repeat from * across.

Row 2: K1, *P1, K1. Repeat from * across.

Repeat Rows 1 and 2 for patt.

NOTES

For fully-fashioned decreases:
on RS rows: K2, P1, K1, SSK, work across in patt as established until 6 sts rem in row, ending row with K2tog, K1, P1, K2; ***on WS rows:*** P1, K3, P2tog, work across in patt as established until 6 sts rem in row, ending row with P2tog *through their back loops,* K3, P1.

SSK = Slip next 2 sts knitwise one at a time, then insert LH needle into the fronts of these 2 sts and knit them tog from this position.

For sweater assembly, refer to the illustration for set-in construction on page 126.

BACK

With A, CO 93 (101, 109, 117, 125) sts. Change to B, beg Textured Rib Patt, and work even until piece measures approx 11¼ (11½, 11¾, 11¾, 11¾)" from beg, ending after WS row.

Shape Armholes

BO 4 sts at the beg of next two rows—85 (93, 101, 109, 117) sts rem.

Work fully-fashioned decreases each side every row 2 (6, 10, 14, 18) times, then every other row 5 (4, 3, 2, 1) times—71 (73, 75, 77, 79) sts rem.

Cont even until piece measures approx 18¾ (19¼, 19¾, 20¼, 20¾)" from beg, ending after WS row.

Shape Shoulders

BO 4 (4, 5, 5, 5) sts each shoulder edge three times, then BO 4 (5, 3, 4, 5) sts each shoulder edge once.

BO rem 39 sts for back of neck.

FRONT

Same as back until piece measures approx 13½ (14, 14½, 15, 15½)" from beg, ending after WS row.

SKILL LEVEL

Advanced Beginner

SIZES

Extra-Small (Small, Medium, Large, Extra-Large). *Instructions are for smallest size, with changes for other sizes noted in parentheses as necessary.*

FINISHED MEASUREMENTS

Bust: 34 (37, 40, 43, 45½)"
Total length: 20 (20½, 21, 21½, 22)"

MATERIALS

Tahki-Stacy Charles/Filatura di Crosa's *Primo* (heavy worsted weight; 100% wool; each approx 1¾ oz/ 50 g and 77 yd/70 m), 1 ball Skipper Blue #255 (A) and 16 (17, 18, 19, 20) balls Fuchsia #121 (B)

One pair of size 9 (5.5 mm) knitting needles or size needed to obtain gauge

16" Circular knitting needle, size 9 (5.5 mm)

7" Zipper

Safety pin

Divide for Zipper Opening

Next Row (RS): Work patt as established across first 35 (36, 37, 38, 39) sts, slip next st onto safety pin for bottom of zipper placket; join second ball of yarn and work patt as established to end row.

Work even on both sides at once with separate balls of yarn until piece measures approx 17 (17½, 18, 18½, 19)" from beg, ending after WS row.

Shape Neck

BO 8 sts each neck edge once, BO 4 sts each neck edge once, then BO 2 sts each neck edge twice—19 (20, 21, 22, 23) sts rem each side.

Dec 1 st each neck edge every row three times—16 (17, 18, 19, 20) sts rem each side.

Cont even until piece measures same as back to shoulders.

Shape Shoulders

Same as for back.

SLEEVES

With A, CO 49 (49, 53, 53, 53) sts. Change to B, beg Textured Rib Patt, and inc 1 st each side every fourth row 0 (0, 0, 0, 5) times, then every sixth row 3 (10, 9, 17, 15) times, then every eighth row 11 (6, 7, 1, 0) times—77 (81, 85, 89, 93) sts.

Cont even until piece measures approx 17½ (17¾, 18, 18, 18)" from beg, ending after WS row.

Shape Cap

BO 4 sts at beg of next two rows—69 (73, 77, 81, 83) sts rem.

Work fully-fashioned decreases each side every other row 2 (2, 3, 5, 4) times, then every row 23 (25, 26, 26, 29) times—19 sts rem.

BO 2 sts at beg of next four rows—11 sts rem.

BO.

FINISHING

Sew shoulder seams.

Neckband

With RS facing, circular needle, and B, pick up and knit 73 sts. Work rows of K1 P1 Rib Patt until band measures approx 3¼" from beg.

Change to A, and work one more row of rib.

BO *loosely* in rib.

Zipper Facing

With RS facing and A, pick up and knit 32 sts along left side of center front opening, knit the one st from safety pin, pick up and knit 32 sts along right side of center front opening.

Next Row: Knit to BO.

Sew in zipper.

Set in sleeves. Sew sleeve and side seams.

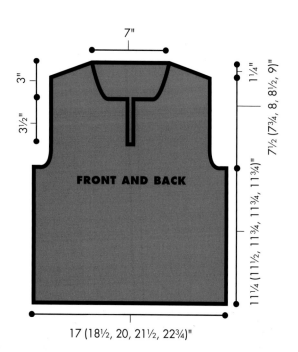

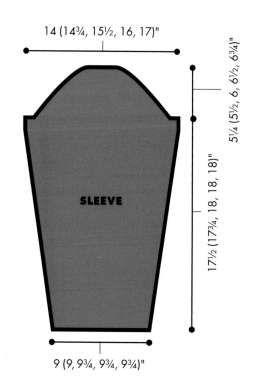

Hannah
Luxuriate in this super-soft alpaca shell. Its subtle interior shaping and deliciously high, ribbed neckband are sexy yet still demure.

GAUGE

In Stockinette St Patt with larger needles, 16 sts and 20 rows = 4". ***To save time, take time to check gauge.***

K1 P1 RIB PATTERN

(over mult. 2 sts)

Row 1 (RS): *K1, P1. Repeat from * across.

Patt Row: *K1, P1. Repeat from * across.

Repeat Patt Row.

STOCKINETTE STITCH PATTERN

(over any number of sts)

Row 1 (RS): Knit across.

Row 2: Purl across.

Repeat Rows 1 and 2 for patt.

NOTES

SSK = Slip next 2 sts knitwise one at a time, then insert LH needle into the fronts of these 2 sts and knit them tog from this position.

M1 = Insert LH needle under the horizontal thread that is between st just worked and the next st, and knit into the back of it.

M1P = Insert LH needle under the horizontal thread that is between st just worked and the next st, and purl into the back of it.

For fully-fashioned raglan decreases: on RS rows: (K1, P1) twice, SSK, knit across until 6 sts rem in row, ending row with K2tog, (P1, K1) twice; ***on WS rows:*** (P1, K1) twice, P2tog, purl across until 6 sts rem in row, ending row with P2tog *through their back loops*, (K1, P1) twice.

BACK

With smaller needles, CO 70 (74, 80, 88, 96) sts. Beg K1 P1 Rib Patt, and work even until piece measures approx 1¼" from beg, ending after WS row.

Change to larger needles, beg Stockinette St Patt, and work even until piece measures approx 3½" from beg, ending after WS row.

Next Row (RS): K20 (22, 25, 29, 33) sts, place marker, SSK, K26 sts, K2tog, place marker, K20 (22, 25, 29, 33) sts to end row.

Work three rows even in Stockinette St Patt.

Next Row (RS): Work to first marker, slip marker, SSK, work until 2 sts before second marker, K2tog, slip marker, work to end row.

Work three rows even in Stockinette St Patt.

Repeat last four rows three more times—60 (64, 70, 78, 86) sts rem.

Remove markers, and work even in Stockinette St Patt until piece measures approx 10 (10, 10¼, 10½, 11)" from beg, ending after WS row.

SKILL LEVEL
Intermediate

SIZES
Extra-Small (Small, Medium, Large, Extra-Large). *Instructions are for smallest size, with changes for other sizes noted in parentheses as necessary.*

FINISHED MEASUREMENTS
Bust: 35 (37, 40, 44, 48)"
Total length: 22½ (22½, 22¾, 23, 23½)"

MATERIALS
JCA/Reynolds's *Alpaca Regal* (heavy worsted weight; 90% alpaca/10% wool; each approx 3½ oz/100 g and 110 yd/100 m), 5 (5, 6, 6, 7) balls Periwinkle #297

One pair each of sizes 8 and 9 (5 and 5.5 mm) knitting needles or size needed to obtain gauge

Stitch holders

Stitch markers

Next Row (RS): K20 (22, 25, 29, 33) sts, place marker, M1, K20 sts, M1, place marker, K20 (22, 25, 29, 33) sts to end row—62 (66, 72, 80, 88) sts.

Work two rows even in Stockinette St Patt.

Next Row (WS): Work to first marker, slip marker, M1P, work across until next marker, M1P, slip marker, work to end row—64 (68, 74, 82, 90) sts.

Work two rows even in Stockinette St Patt.

Next Row (RS): Work to first marker, slip marker, M1, work across until next marker, M1, slip marker, work to end row—66 (70, 76, 84, 92) sts.

Repeat last six rows two more times—70 (74, 80, 88, 96) sts.

Cont even in Stockinette St Patt until piece measures approx 15½ (15, 15¼, 15, 15½)" from beg, ending after WS row.

Shape Armholes

Work fully-fashioned raglan decreases every row 0 (0, 4, 10, 18) times, every other row 14 (17, 17, 15, 11) times, then every fourth row 2 (1, 0, 0, 0) times—38 sts rem.

BO 5 sts at beg of next two rows—28 sts rem.

Slip sts onto holder.

FRONT

Same as back until piece measures approx 20 (20, 20¼, 20½, 21)" from beg, ending after WS row.

Cont fully-fashioned raglan decreases same as back, *and at the same time,* slip middle 14 sts onto holder.

Work both sides at once with separate balls of yarn,

and dec 1 st each neck edge every other row seven times—5 sts rem each side.

BO.

FINISHING

Sew right shoulder seam.

Neckband

With RS facing and smaller needles, pick up and knit 68 sts around neckline, including sts from holders. Work even in K1 P1 Rib Patt until band measures approx 3¾" from beg.

BO *loosely* in rib.

Sew left shoulder seam, including side of neckband.

Sew side seams.

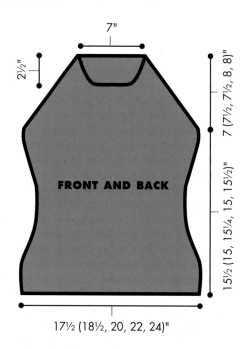

FRONT AND BACK

7"

2½"

7 (7½, 7½, 8, 8)"

15½ (15, 15¼, 15, 15½)"

17½ (18½, 20, 22, 24)"

Megan

Think "sexy" always means "bare"? This winter warmer might change your mind! Knit sideways, its funky, fringed lower edge is created as you go, making finishing a breeze.

GAUGE

In Basketweave Patt, 23 sts and 32 rows = 4". *To save time, take time to check gauge.*

LOWER CABLE PANEL

(over 34 sts)
See chart on page 117.

BASKETWEAVE PATTERN

(over mult. 6 + 2 sts)
See chart on page 117.

NECKBAND CABLE PANEL

(over 26 sts)
See chart on page 117.

NOTES

To create the lower fringe, 7 sts are unraveled all the way to the cast-on edge; to secure the top of the fringe, make overhand knots as close to the knitted fabric as possible.

Constructionwise, the cabled neckband is worked separately and is sewn onto the neckline sideways.

To do a knit-on cast-on, *insert RH needle into the first stitch on the LH needle, knit up a stitch and immediately transfer it back to the LH needle. Repeat from * until the required number of stitches is cast on.

For sweater assembly, refer to the illustration for set-in construction on page 126.

BACK

Sideways Cable Panel

Using knit-on technique, CO 34 sts. Beg Lower Cable Panel, and work even until piece measures approx 18 (20, 22¼, 24½, 26½)" from beg, ending after WS row.

Create Fringe

Next Row (RS): BO first 27 sts; unravel rem 7 sts all the way down to the cast-on edge and all along the edge. Cut the loops, and using overhand knots, tie two strands tog into each group. Trim fringe evenly.

With RS facing, pick up and knit 104 (116, 128, 140, 152) sts evenly along side edge of cabled piece opposite fringe.

Beg Basketweave Patt, and work even until piece measures approx 9½ (9½, 9½, 9½, 10)" from beg, ending after WS row.

Shape Armholes

BO 3 (4, 5, 5, 6) sts at beg of next two rows—98 (108, 118, 130, 140) sts rem.

SKILL LEVEL

Intermediate

SIZES

Small (Medium, Large, Extra-Large, Extra-Extra Large). *Instructions are for smallest size, with changes for other sizes noted in parentheses as necessary.*

FINISHED MEASUREMENTS

Bust: 36 (40, 44½, 49, 53)"
Total length (excluding fringe): 18 (18¼, 18½, 19, 20)"

MATERIALS

Paton's *Classic Wool* (worsted weight; 100% wool; each approx 3½ oz/100 g and 223 yd/204 m), 7 (7, 8, 8, 9) balls Peacock #218

One pair of size 7 (4.5 mm) knitting needles or size needed to obtain gauge

Cable needle

Shape Shoulders

BO 5 (5, 5, 5, 6) sts each shoulder edge three times, then BO 4 (5, 5, 6, 4) sts each shoulder edge once.

BO rem 40 sts for back of neck.

FRONT

Same as back until piece measures approx 15½ (15¾, 16, 16½, 17½)" from beg, ending after WS row.

Shape Neck

Next Row (RS): Work across first 31 (32, 32, 33, 34) sts; join second ball of yarn and BO middle 16 sts, work to end row.

Work both sides at once with separate balls of yarn and BO 3 sts each neck edge twice, then BO 2 sts each neck edge once—23 (24, 24, 25, 26) sts rem each side.

Dec 1 st each neck edge every row twice, then every other row twice—19 (20, 20, 21, 22) sts rem each side.

Cont even, if necessary, until piece measures same as back to shoulders, ending after WS row.

Shape Shoulders

Same as for back.

SLEEVES

CO 50 sts. Beg with Row 3, work even in Basketweave Patt until piece measures approx 1" from beg, ending after WS row.

BO 2 (2, 3, 4, 4) sts at beg of next two (two, two, four, four) rows—94 (104, 112, 114, 124) sts rem.

Dec 1 st each side every row 0 (2, 6, 6, 12) times, then every other row 4 (9, 10, 10, 8) times, then every fourth row 4 (1, 0, 0, 0) times—78 (80, 80, 82, 84) sts rem.

Cont even in patt as established until piece measures approx 17 (17¼, 17½, 18, 19)" from beg, ending after WS row.

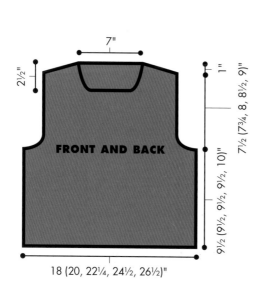

FRONT AND BACK

2½"

7"

1"

7½ (7¾, 8, 8½, 9)"

9½ (9½, 9½, 9½, 10)"

18 (20, 22¼, 24½, 26½)"

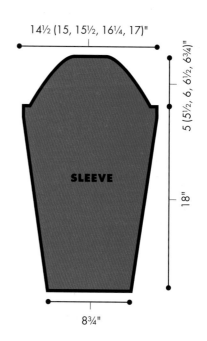

SLEEVE

14½ (15, 15½, 16¼, 17)"

5 (5½, 6, 6½, 6¾)"

18"

8¾"

Inc 1 st each side on next row and then every fourth row 0 (0, 0, 1, 7) times, every sixth row 3 (7, 15, 20, 16) times, then every eighth row 13 (10, 4, 0, 0) times—84 (86, 90, 94, 98) sts.

Cont even until piece measures approx 18" from beg, ending after WS row.

Shape Cap

BO 3 (4, 5, 5, 6) sts at beg of next two rows—78 (78, 80, 84, 86) sts rem.

Dec 1 st each side every other row 5 (9, 12, 14, 15) times, then every row 24 (20, 18, 18, 18) times—20 sts rem.

BO 2 sts at beg of next four rows.

BO rem 12 sts.

HOT TIP

For even more fun, add beads or macramé to your fringe!

FINISHING

Sew shoulder seams.

Neckband

CO 26 sts. Work Neckband Cable Panel until piece, when slightly stretched, fits around neckline of sweater. BO. Sew neckband onto neckline, sewing cast-on and bind-off edges tog at center back of neck.

Set in sleeves. Sew sleeve and side seams.

LOWER CABLE PANEL

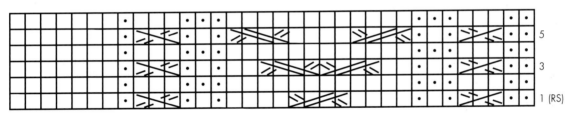

34 sts

NECKBAND CABLE PANEL

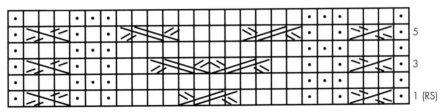

26 sts

BASKETWEAVE PATTERN

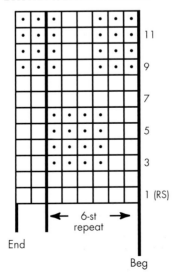

KEY

☐ = K on RS; P on WS

• = P on RS; K on WS

= Slip 2 sts onto cn and hold in back; K1; K2 from cn

= Slip next st onto cn and hold in front; K2; K st from cn

= Slip next 2 sts onto cn and hold in front; K2; K2 from cn

= Slip 2 sts onto cn and hold in back; K2; K2 from cn

Julia

A multicolored, harvest-hued ribbon yarn is all it takes to make this design unforgettable. And easy fisherman rib and self-finished edges make it a snap to knit!

GAUGE

In Fisherman Rib Patt with straight needles, 13 sts and 24 rows = 4". **To save time, take time to check gauge.**

FISHERMAN RIB PATTERN

(over mult. 2 + 1 sts)

Row 1 (WS): Knit across.

Row 2: P1, *knit next st *in the row below,* P1. Repeat from * across.

Repeat Rows 1 and 2 for patt.

NOTES

Throughout, instructions include one selvage st each side; these sts are not reflected in final measurements.

SSSK = Slip next 3 sts knitwise one at a time, then insert LH needle into the fronts of these 3 sts and knit them tog from this position.

BACK

With straight needles, CO 55 (59, 63, 67, 71) sts. Beg Fisherman Rib Patt, and work even until piece measures approx 12 (12, 12, 12½, 12½)" from beg, ending after RS row.

Shape Armholes

Next Row (WS): K5, P1, K1, P1, knit across until 8 sts rem in row, ending row with P1, K1, P1, K5.

Next Row: (P1, K1) twice, P1, SSSK, work Row 2 of Fisherman Rib Patt across until 8 sts rem in row, ending row with K3tog, (P1, K1) twice, P1— 51 (55, 59, 63, 67) sts rem.

Next Row: Knit across.

Next Row: P1, *knit next st *in the row below,* P1. Repeat from * across.

Repeat last four rows 2 (3, 3, 4, 4) more times—43 (43, 47, 47, 51) sts rem.

Cont even until piece measures approx 18½ (19, 19½, 20½, 20½)" from beg, ending after WS row.

SKILL LEVEL

Intermediate

SIZES

Extra-Small (Small, Medium, Large, Extra-Large). *Instructions are for smallest size, with changes for other sizes noted in parentheses as necessary.*

FINISHED MEASUREMENTS

Bust: 33 (35, 37½, 40, 42½)"
Total length: 20 (20½, 21, 22, 22)"

MATERIALS

Knit One Crochet Too's *Tartelette* (heavy worsted weight; 50% cotton/40% Tactel® nylon/10% nylon; each approx 1¾ oz/50 g and 75 yd/68 m), 7 (8, 9, 10, 10) hanks of Golden Plum #471

One pair of straight size 9 (5.5 mm) knitting needles or size needed to obtain gauge

16" Circular knitting needles, sizes 9 and 10 (5.5 and 6 mm)

Work both sides at once with separate balls of yarn, and BO 2 sts each neck edge twice—13 (13, 15, 15, 17) sts rem each side.

Dec 1 st each neck edge every other row twice—11 (11, 13, 13, 15) sts rem each side.

Cont even until piece measures same as back to shoulders, ending after WS row.

Shape Shoulders
Same as for back.

FINISHING
Sew shoulder seams.

Neckband
With RS facing and smaller circular needle, pick up and knit 56 sts around neckline. Join.

Rnd 1: *Knit next st *in the row below*, P1. Repeat from * around.

Rnd 2: Knit.

Repeat Rnds 1 and 2 until band measures approx 4" from beg.

Change to larger circular needle, and cont in patt as established until band measures approx 9" from beg.

BO *loosely*.

Sew side seams.

Shape Shoulders
BO 3 (3, 3, 3, 4) sts each shoulder edge three times, then BO 2 (2, 4, 4, 3) sts each shoulder edge once.

BO rem 21 sts for back of neck.

FRONT
Same as back until piece measures approx 16½ (17, 17½, 18½, 18½)" from beg, ending after WS row.

Shape Neck
Next Row (RS): Work patt as established across first 17 (17, 19, 19, 21) sts; join second ball of yarn and BO middle 9 sts, work to end row.

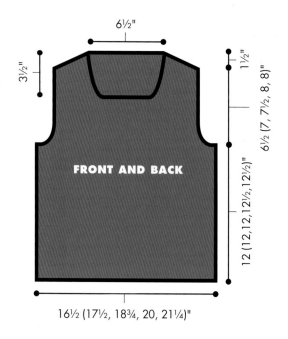

6½"

3½"

1½"

6½ (7, 7½, 8, 8)"

FRONT AND BACK

12 (12, 12, 12½, 12½)"

16½ (17½, 18¾, 20, 21¼)"

Kelly

Wear your heart where it belongs! Here, sensuous and soft angora-blended yarn hints at your romantic nature.

GAUGE

In Seed St Patt with larger needles, 20 sts and 32 rows = 4". **To save time, take time to check gauge.**

K2 P2 RIB PATTERN

(over mult. 4 + 2 sts)

Row 1 (RS): K2, *P2, K2. Repeat from * across.

Row 2: P2, *K2, P2. Repeat from * across.

Repeat Rows 1 and 2 for patt.

SEED STITCH PATTERN

(over mult. 2 + 1 sts)

Patt Row: P1, *K1, P1. Repeat from * across.

Repeat Patt Row.

STOCKINETTE STITCH PATTERN

(over any number of sts)

Row 1 (RS): Knit across.

Row 2: Purl across.

Repeat Rows 1 and 2 for patt.

HEART MEDALLION PATTERN

(over middle 23 sts, increases to 31 sts)

See chart on page 124.

NOTES

M1 = Insert LH needle under the horizontal thread that is between st just worked and the next st, and knit into the back of it.

SSK = Slip next 2 sts knitwise one at a time, then insert LH needle into the fronts of these 2 sts and knit them tog from this position.

For fully-fashioned decreases:
on RS rows: K1, SSK, work across in patt as established until 3 sts rem in row, ending row with K2tog, K1;
on WS rows: P1, P2tog, work across in patt as established until 3 sts rem in row, ending row with P2tog *through their back loops,* P1.

Once first decrease row has been worked, maintain 2 sts in Stockinette St Patt each side.

For sweater assembly, refer to the illustration for set-in construction on page 126.

SKILL LEVEL
Advanced

SIZES
Small (Medium, Large, Extra-Large, Extra-Extra Large). *Instructions are for smallest size, with changes for other sizes noted in parentheses as necessary.*

FINISHED MEASUREMENTS
Bust: 37 (40, 42, 44½, 47)"
Total length: 21½ (22, 22½, 23, 23½)"

MATERIALS
Classic Elite's *Lush* (worsted weight; 50% angora/50% wool; each approx 1¾ oz/ 50 g and 123 yd/113 m), 12 (13, 13, 14, 15) hanks Seafoam #4420

One pair each of sizes 6 and 7 (4 and 4.5 mm) knitting needles or size needed to obtain gauge

Cable needle

Next Row (RS): Change to larger needles, beg Seed St Patt, and inc 1 st each side every twenty-second (sixteenth, twenty-second, sixteenth, tenth) row 1 (2, 1, 2, 3) times, working new sts into Seed St Patt—93 (99, 105, 111, 117) sts.

Cont even until piece measures approx 13 (13¼, 13½, 13½, 13½)" from beg, ending after WS row.

Shape Armholes

Next Row (RS): BO 3 (4, 4, 5, 7) sts at beg of next two rows. BO 2 (2, 3, 3, 3) sts at beg of next two rows—83 (87, 91, 95, 97) sts rem.

Work fully-fashioned decreases each side every row 1 (3, 3, 2, 2) times, then every other row 6 (5, 7, 9, 9) times—69 (71, 71, 73, 75) sts rem.

Cont even, maintaining 2 selvage sts each side in Stockinette St Patt with Seed St Patt over all other sts until piece measures approx 20½ (21, 21½, 22, 22½)" from beg, ending after WS row.

Shape Shoulders

BO 4 (4, 4, 5, 5) sts each shoulder edge three times, then BO 5 (6, 6, 4, 5) sts each shoulder edge once.

BO rem 35 sts for back of neck.

FRONT

Same as back until piece measures approx 13 (13¼, 13¾, 14¼, 14¾)" from beg, ending after WS row.

Set Up Medallion Patt

Next Row (RS): Cont armhole decreases same as back, work Row 1 of Heart Medallion Patt over middle 23 sts, keeping all other sts in patts as established.

BACK

With smaller needles, CO 90 (94, 102, 106, 110) sts. Beg K2 P2 Rib Patt, and work even until piece measures approx 7½ (7½, 8, 8, 8)" from beg, ending after RS row.

Next Row (WS): P2, M1, *K2, P2. Repeat from * across—91 (95, 103, 107, 111) sts.

FRONT AND BACK

2½"

7"

1"

7½ (7¾, 8, 8½, 9)"

13 (13¼, 13½, 13½, 13½)"

18½ (20, 21, 22¼, 23½)"

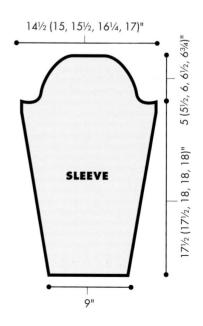

SLEEVE

14½ (15, 15½, 16¼, 17)"

5 (5½, 6, 6½, 6¾)"

17½ (17½, 18, 18, 18)"

9"

After Row 38 of Heart Medallion Patt has been completed, cont even, keeping 2 selvage sts each side in Stockinette St Patt with Seed St Patt over all other sts, until piece measures approx 19 (19½, 20, 20½, 21)" from beg, ending after WS row.

Shape Neck

Next Row (RS): Work patt as established across first 28 (29, 29, 30, 31) sts; join second ball of yarn and BO middle 13 sts, cont patt as established to end row.

Work both sides at once with separate balls of yarn, and BO 3 sts each neck edge once, then BO 2 sts each neck edge once.

Work fully-fashioned decreases each neck edge every row six times—17 (18, 18, 19, 20) sts rem each side.

Cont even until piece measures same as back to shoulders, ending after WS row.

Shape Shoulders

Same as for back.

SLEEVES

With smaller needles, CO 46 sts. Beg K2 P2 Rib Patt, and work even until piece measures approx 1" from beg, ending after RS row.

Next Row (WS): P2, M1, *K2, P2. Repeat from * across—47 sts.

Change to larger needles, beg Seed St Patt, and inc 1 st each side every sixth row 0 (0, 0, 4, 12) times, then every eighth row 3 (8, 11, 13, 7) times, then every tenth row 10 (6, 4, 0, 0) times—73 (75, 77, 81, 85) sts. Work even until piece measures approx 17½ (17½, 18, 18, 18)" from beg, ending after WS row.

Shape Cap

BO 3 (4, 4, 5, 7) sts at beg of next two rows—67 (67, 69, 71, 71) sts rem.

Work fully-fashioned decreases each side every other row 10 (14, 17, 20, 22) times, then every row 14 (10, 8, 6, 4) times—19 sts rem.

BO 2 sts at beg of next four rows.

BO rem 11 sts.

FINISHING

Sew right shoulder seam.

Neckband

With RS facing and smaller needles, pick up and knit 94 sts around neckline. Beg with Row 2 of K2 P2 Rib Patt, work even until band measures approx 4½" from beg. Change to larger needles, and cont even in K2 P2 Rib Patt until band measures approx 9" from beg.

BO *loosely* in rib.

Sew left shoulder seam, including side of neckband.

Set in sleeves. Sew sleeve and side seams.

HEART MEDALLION PATTERN

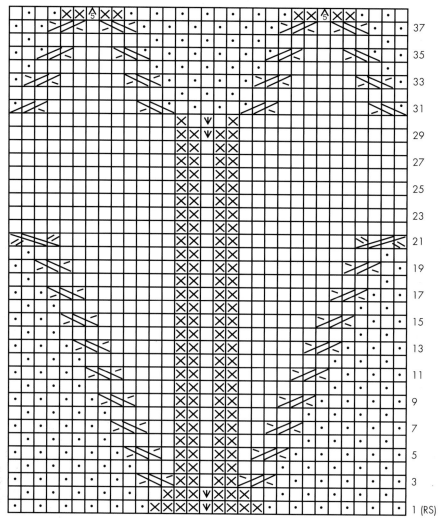

Middle 23 sts (increases to 31 sts)

KEY

• = P on RS; K on WS

□ = K on RS; P on WS

✕ = No stitch

Ⅴ = Central Double Increase (increases from 1 to 3 sts) = On RS rows: Knit into back and then into front of indicated st and slip them off LH needle onto RH needle; insert point of LH needle behind the vertical strand that runs downward between the two sts just made, and knit into the back of it; on WS rows: P into (back, front, back) of st

⟋⟋⟍ = Slip next st onto cn and hold in back; K2; K1 from cn

⟍⟍⟍ = Slip next 2 sts onto cn and hold in front; K1; K2 from cn

⟹⟍⟍ = Slip next 2 sts onto cn and hold in back; K2; K2 from cn

⟹⟍⟍ = Slip next 2 sts onto cn and hold in front: K2; K2 from cn

⟍⟍• = Slip next 2 sts onto cn and hold in front; P1; K2 from cn

•⟋⟍ = Slip next st onto cn and hold in back; K2; P1 from cn

⚡₅ = Slip next 3 sts with yarn in back, drop yarn; *pass the second st on RH needle over the first st on RH needle; slip first st from RH needle back to LH needle; pass the second st on LH needle over the first st on LH needle**; slip first st from LH needle back to RH needle and repeat from * to ** once again; pick up yarn and P remaining st

Sweater Assembly

Pieces for knitted garments fit together like a jigsaw puzzle, with the type of armhole determining how the front, back, and sleeves interlock. Refer to these drawings when assembling sweaters.

SQUARE INDENTED   **RAGLAN**   **SET-IN**

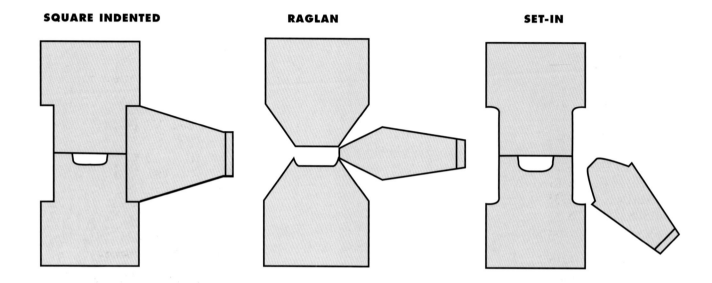

Yarn Choice and Substitution

Each project in this collection was designed with a specific yarn in mind. Due to unique characteristics such as fiber content, twist, texture, and thickness, every yarn appears and behaves differently when knitted. For the best results, I recommend that you use the suggested yarn.

If you would like to make a yarn substitution, be sure to choose one whose weight matches the one designated in the pattern. Knit a test swatch with the yarn you prefer, using the needle size suggested on the ball band, and count the number of stitches over 4 inches. Use this table to determine its weight.

Before beginning any project, take time to knit a piece of the fabric actually called for in the pattern, and measure your gauge. Use whatever knitting needle size you require to obtain the specified gauge.

YARN WEIGHT	STITCHES PER 4"
Fingering weight	24 or more
Sport weight	22-24
Light worsted weight	20-22
Worsted weight	19-20
Heavy worsted weight	16-18
Bulky weight	15 or fewer

Material Resources

Manufacturers (*These companies sell wholesale only. Contact them to locate retail stores in your area.*)

Aurora Yarns
2385 Carlos Street
P.O. Box 3068
Moss Beach, CA 94038
(650) 728-8554
www.garnstudio.com

Berroco Yarns
Elmdale Road
P.O. Box 367
Uxbridge, MA 01569
(508) 278-2527
www.berroco.com

Brown Sheep Company
100662 County Road 16
Mitchell, NE 69357
(308) 635-2198
www.brownsheep.com

Cherry Tree Hill Yarn
52 Church Street
Barton, VT 05822
(802) 525-3311

Classic Elite Yarns
300-A Jackson Street
Lowell, MA 01852
(978) 453-2837

Filatura di Crosa
(*See* Tahki/Stacy Charles)

Jaeger Yarns
(*See* Westminster Fibers)

JCA, Inc.
35 Scales Lane
Townsend, MA 01469
(978) 597-8794

JHB International, Inc.
1955 South Quince Street
Denver, CO 80231
(303) 751-8100
www.buttons.com

Knit One Crochet Too, Inc.
7 Commons Avenue
Suite 2
Windham, ME 04062
(207) 892-9625
www.knitonecrochettoo.com

Lane Borgosesia
16742 Stagg Street
#104
Van Nuys, CA 91406
(818) 780-5497

Lion Brand Yarn
34 West 15th Street
New York, NY 10011
(212) 243-8995
www.lionbrand.com

Muench Yarns
285 Bel Marin Keys
#J
Novato, CA 94949
(415) 883-6375
www.muenchyarns.com

One World Button Supply
   Company
41 Union Square West
Room 311
New York, NY 10003
(212) 691-1331
www.oneworldbuttons.com

Patons Yarns
320 Livingstone Avenue South
Listowel, Ontario N4W 3H3
Canada
(519) 291-3780
www.patonsyarns.com

Rowan Yarns
(*See* Westminster Fibers)

Skacel Collection, Inc.
P.O. Box 88110
Seattle, WA 98168
(253) 854-2710

S. R. Kertzer Ltd.
105 A Winges Road
Woodbridge, Ontario L4L 6C2
Canada
(905) 856-3447
www.kertzer.com

Tahki/Stacy Charles
8000 Cooper Avenue
Building I
Glendale, NY 11385
(718) 326-4433
www.tahkistacycharles.com

Westminster Fibers
4 Townsend West
Suite #8
Nashua, NH 03063
(603) 886-5041
www.knitrowan.com

Mail Order and Internet Yarn Sources

Herrschner's and Herrschner's
   Yarn Shoppe
2800 Hoover Road
Stevens Point, WI 54492
(800) 441-0838
www.herrschners.com

Patternworks
Route 25
P.O. Box 1618
Center Harbor, NH 03226
(800) 438-5464
www.patternworks.com

Wool Connection
34 East Main Street
Avon, CT 06001
(800) 933-9665
www.woolconnection.com

Instructional Resources

The patterns in this book assume a working knowledge of basic knitting techniques. For additional technical information, refer to one of the following books:

Allen, Pam. *Knitting for Dummies.* New York: Wiley Publishing, 2002.

Goldberg, Rhoda Ochser. *The New Knitting Dictionary, 1000 Stitches and Patterns.* New York: Crown, 1984.

Hiatt, June Hemmons. *The Principles of Knitting.* New York: Simon and Schuster, 1989.

Melville, Sally. *The Knit Stitch (The Knitting Experience, Book 1).* Sioux Falls, SD: XRX Books, 2002.

Mountford, Debra, ed. *The Harmony Guide to Knitting Techniques and Stitches.* New York: Harmony, 1992.

Righetti, Maggie. *Knitting in Plain English.* New York: St. Martins Press, 1986.

Stanley, Montse. *The Reader's Digest Guide to Knitting.* Pleasantville, NY: Reader's Digest, 1993.

Swartz, Judith L. *Hip to Knit.* Loveland, CO: Interweave Press, 2002.

Thomas, Mary. *Mary Thomas's Knitting Book.* London: Hodder and Stoughton, Ltd., 1943. Reprint. New York: Dover, 1973.

Thomas, Nancy J., and Ilana Rabinowitz. *A Passion for Knitting.* New York: Fireside, 2002.

Vogue Knitting editors. *Vogue Knitting, The Ultimate Knitting Book.* Updated ed. New York: Sixth and Spring Books, 2002.

Index